mini
Bahrain
The Essential **Visitors'** Guide

In association with

Bahrain mini Explorer
ISBN 13 – 978-9948-03-319-6
ISBN 10 – 9948-03-319-1

Copyright © Explorer Group Ltd 2007
All rights reserved.

All maps © Explorer Group Ltd 2007

Front cover photograph: Painted Village – Victor Romero

Printed and bound by
Emirates Printing Press, Dubai, UAE

Explorer Publishing & Distribution
PO Box 34275
Dubai , United Arab Emirates
Phone (+971 4) 340 8805 **Fax** (+971 4) 340 8806
Email info@explorerpublishing.com
Web www.explorerpublishing.com

The Kingdom of Bahrain may be the smallest country in the Gulf, but it is jam-packed with heritage, culture, buzzing nightlife and the warmest of welcomes. From the bustling capital of Manama to the remote beaches on the Hawar Islands – you'll find it all covered in this guide. Small enough to fit in your pocket, but packing a big, informative punch, this mini marvel is written by residents of Bahrain and covers everything from visas (p.11) and local knowledge (p.14), to restaurant and bar reviews (p.120) and the lowdown on where to go and what to see all over the island (p.34).

Introduction

The Explorer Team

Contents

Essentials

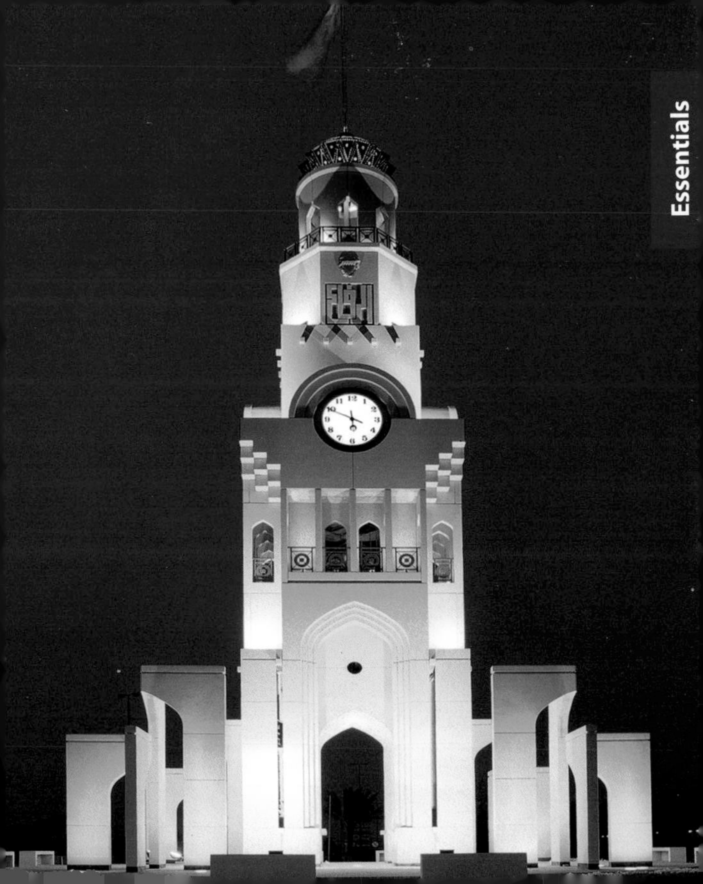

Island Of Golden Smiles

Old world charm merges with new world buzz in one of the most unique and exciting kingdoms in the Gulf.

In Bahrain you'll experience a kingdom of contrasts; old and new, luxury and tradition, sprawling desert and towering structures, historical scenes and modern architecture. Known for its hospitality, it represents a fascinating blend of traditional Arab and western cultures and, unlike many of its regional neighbours, it has a large local population living alongside its expatriate residents.

While not yet viewed internationally as a tourist destination, the kingdom is truly an undiscovered gem and the government is working hard for recognition in travellers' minds. As a visitor to the island this is great news for you; take advantage of the burgeoning infrastructure, inexpensive nightlife and new hotels.

While a little cliched, it is the people of Bahrain and their pride in their home country that sets the place apart from its neighbours; warm welcomes and genuinely friendly service are all part of life here. While the atmosphere in the capital of Manama can be a little frenetic - which isn't helped by the driving - there's a pretty laid back vibe with little animosity between the various groups in society. This means that Bahrain is one of the safest destinations you can visit and crimes don't happen often. Women may get some unwanted attention and while it is very rarely threatening, if this is your first visit to the Middle East, it can take time to get used to it.

Bahrain is made up of 33 islands, including some manmade, with the main island being relatively small (a mere 586.5 square kilometres), so you can travel the length within an hour and despite the frequently changing roads, the capital Manama is fairly easy to navigate. This means you can get your bearings within a day and then feel like a local for the rest of your stay. Don't be afraid to get lost though, often this can be the best way to stumble upon a slice of the true Bahrain.

Once you are settled there is a wealth of activities, attractions, shops and nightlife, not to mention shameless relaxation, to keep you occupied. There is an unfortunate lack of beaches, but if you're after a holiday doing nothing you probably would have chosen somewhere else.

Bahrain's ancient past and ambitious future mean that your days will be packed - after the world-class exhibits at the National Museum and driving at the International Circuit your head will be spinning, so it's lucky there are some amazing restaurants and spas to help you to unwind.

When night falls and hunger strikes, your only problem could be too much choice; the cuisines on offer reflect Bahrain's multi-cultural population so take your pick. Eating out is usually quite inexpensive but for a really special night it is, of course, easy to find an upmarket restaurant to relieve you of some funds. After dinner head to a club for some live music, Arabic house or a western style night out.

A visit to Bahrain is an unexpected delight, whether staying with friends or exploring from your hotel. It's a financial hub, an expat playground and an ideal choice for a minibreak - so read this book, plan your time and enjoy.

Visitors' Checklist

Bahrain International Circuit

With year round events including drag racing and rally driving as well as the famed F1 Grand Prix, this stunning venue is perfect for action fans. Take a tour of the site or just watch the experts do their thing, see page 77.

Spas

Spoil yourself at a world-class spa. The Ritz-Carlton (p.102) in Seef and the new Banyan Tree Desert Resort & Spa (p.101) right, near Al Areen Wildlife Park will pamper you in every possible way, all in stunning surroundings.

Forts

An action-packed past has resulted in some impressive forts all over the kingdom. The sites at Riffa (p.79), Arad (p.70) and Bahrain Fort near Karabad Village, (p.62) are all excellent examples where you can learn more.

Art Galleries

There is an abundance of art galleries all over the island. Of particular note are La Fontaine (p.51) right, with its exhibitions in cool corridors, and Arabesque Art Gallery (p.48) for buying smaller pieces.

Beach Clubs

Despite being an island, Bahrain has only a few good beaches, so try the man-made efforts like the stunning sweep of sand at the Ritz-Carlton (p.59) right, and the water sports haven at the Novotel Al Dana Resort (p.52).

An Evening In Adliya

Haggle in the dozens of shops lining the main street before dining at one of the many restaurants, such as Mezzaluna (p.144) pictured right, then finish with shisha on the terrace at one of the cafes or a drink at JJs (p.150).

Boat Trips

Cut through the waves on a speedboat or sail away on a dhow – the choice is yours. From exciting dolphin watching to jetskiing (see Watersports & Diving on page 96), there is an on-board adventure to suit everyone.

Traditional Handicrafts

Visit villages to see local handicrafts; the pottery at Al A'ali, cloth weaving at Bani Jamrah and basket weaving at Barbar. Jewellery, iron, wood and calligraphy are also on display at Al Jasrah Handicraft Centre (p.76).

Museums

The island has a rich history which is celebrated through several museums. Bahrain National Museum (p.48) right, on the corniche attracts world-class exhibits while the Oil Museum (p.78) offers a fascinating insight into the industry.

Beit Al Qur'an

This is quite simply a must-see. From the stunning engravings on the exterior to the stained glass dome, this museum is enchanting. Displaying rare Islamic artwork, it is a true treat for the eyes and mind – the free entry is a bonus too, see page 48.

Souks

Get your haggling hat on at one of Manama's souks where you'll experience traditional Middle Eastern shopping. Buy anything and everything at Manama Souk (p.115), head to Gold City (p.115) for jewellery or sniff out the spices at the food market.

Al Fateh Mosque

Accommodating up to 7,000 people at prayer, this is Bahrain's largest mosque. Non-Muslims can take tours and it is particularly worth a visit during Eid when there are educational talks, calligraphy and henna painting, see page 90.

Essentials

Visitors' Checklist

Visiting Bahrain

As long as you're careful about the contents of your luggage, entry into Bahrain is easy and straightforward.

Getting There

Bahrain is served by one international airport, situated on the island of Muharraq, around 10 minutes drive from Manama city centre. It has lots of cheap parking, some reasonable restaurants, a large duty-free and several shops, but you would be hard pushed to be entertained there for any serious length of time if delayed. Several 'budget' airlines including Jazeera Airways and Air Arabia have added Bahrain to their destination schedules making it easier to travel there from elsewhere in the Middle East. For airlines flying into Bahrain, see the table on the opposite page.

E-tickets & Electronic Check-in

Many airlines issue e-tickets which you then produce with your passport at the check-in desk, however the use of smart cards or e-gate services is not currently applicable.

Airport Transport

There is no dedicated airport bus service in Bahrain but all the major hotels provide their own transport service, and there will often be a modest fee (no more than BD 5) for the transfer. Taxis are readily available from outside the Arrivals terminal and a journey into Manama should cost no more than BD 3, or see the table on p.25 for details of car hire.

Visas

Citizens of the GCC countries (Saudi Arabia, the UAE, Kuwait, Qatar and Oman) do not require visas to enter Bahrain. Citizens of 35 countries, which include the USA, Canada, Japan, New Zealand, most EU countries, Norway and Switzerland, can obtain a tourist visa on arrival at the airport for BD 5; it is advisable to have dinars on hand but other currencies will be accepted. Citizens from all other countries

Airlines		
Air Arabia	www.airarabia.com	1750 5111
Air India	www.airindia.com	1722 3850
American Airlines	www.aa.com	1753 1000
British Airways	www.britishairways.com	1758 7777
Cathay Pacific	www.cathaypacific.com	1722 6226
Cyprus Airways	www.cyprusairways.com	1722 0849
Egypt Air	www.egyptair.com.eg	1720 9264
Emirates	www.emirates.com	1758 8700
Gulf Air	www.gulfair.com	1772 2200
Iran Air	www.iranair.com	1721 0414
Jazeera Airways	www.jazeeraairways.com	1732 9301
KLM	www.klm.com	1722 9747
Kuwait Airways	www.kuwait-airways.com	1721 2299
Lufthansa	www.lufthansa.com	1782 8761
Oman Air	www.oman-air.com	1750 0020
Qatar Airways	www.qatarairways.com	1721 2277
Yemen Airways	www.yemenia.com	1722 3181

require visas from the appropriated embassy prior to arrival, while British passport holders will automatically receive a three month visa at the airport. For full details visit the Ministry of Immigration's website, www.evisa.gov.bh, where you can check requirements for every nationality.

Customs

At the airport all bags are checked electronically and some are checked manually either at random or if an item arouses suspicion. Forbidden items include firearms, items produced in Israel, pornographic material, drugs, ivory and cultured pearls. Codeine is a banned substance in Bahrain so if you are taking any medication containing it make sure you have a doctor's note.

The duty free allowances are generally two litres of spirits, two litres of wine, and 2,000 cigarettes, but allowances differ depending on which country the visitor is coming from. Visitors are advised to check allowances on www.bdutyfree.com before travelling.

Over The Causeway

People in transit to Saudi Arabia via the causeway should note that no pork products, alcohol, pornographic material (which can include seemingly innocuous items such as underwear adverts in women's magazines, or family beach photographs), or non-Muslim religious objects or literature are allowed across the border and the consequences for attempting to bring them in can be severe.

Clockwise from top left: Al Khamis Mosque, Shaikh Isa Bin Ali House, University of Bahrain

Local Knowledge

It's always best to be prepared – read on for essential information you should know while in Bahrain.

Apart from this book, your hotel concierge or your hosts are the best bets when planning your stay; many hotel lobbies have information points with leaflets on how to spend your day, and you can't beat the recommendation of a trusted friend. There are tourist information offices in the Diplomatic Area and in Bab Al Bahrain (p.42) on Government Avenue; there you can buy the usual souvenirs, postcards, maps and some handicrafts. The official (recently revamped) website is www.bahrain.com. Remember to pick up copies of local papers and magazines for listings of one-off events and activities – DJs, performers, artists and exhibitions all visit Bahrain, so keep up to date if you don't want to miss out.

Climate

The summer in Bahrain can get extremely hot and humid. From June to September temperatures average 35°C (97°F) during the day, sometimes reaching 48°C at the height of summer. From November to April the weather is much more pleasant, with warm days and cool nights. Temperatures at this time range from 15°C to 24°C. The coolest months of the year are generally December and January, when the island experiences northern winds, and at night the temperature sometimes drops to 10°C. Be aware that cinemas and shopping malls can often be a little over generous with the air conditioning so take an extra layer.

Time

The local time is +3hrs UCT (Universal Coordinated Time, formerly GMT). Weekends changed recently to Friday and Saturday to be more in keeping with international business. Shops are generally open from 09:00 to 19:00 and shopping malls open to 22:00 but often stores close for a three hour lunch. In general, local people get up early, have an afternoon siesta, then stay up and eat late in the evening.

Dos & Don'ts

As a guest in a Muslim country you should respect the laws and customs. The 'do' part is easy; do make an effort to see what Bahrain has to offer. It is a unique place in the Gulf, with a particular charm and culture. The 'don'ts' are also simple: don't break the law. Drugs are illegal, as is pornography and prostitution. Driving after having consumed alcohol, any at all, is illegal. The Islamic culture does not encourage public displays of affection between the sexes and male visitors should never offer to shake the hand of a Bahraini woman, or touch her in any way. In general, the best guide is an appreciation of the cultural sensitivities and a dose of common sense.

Tipping

In restaurants there is a service charge of 15% added but tipping is expected on top of this, which should go direct to your waiter or waitress. In bars and clubs it's not necessary to tip bar staff but it might ensure quicker service for the night. As for taxis, it's best to round up to the nearest BD.

Crime & Safety

The crime rate in Bahrain has historically been very low and it is often one of the first things that visitors and new residents comment on. However, it has risen in the last few years, particularly petty crime against low-income foreign workers and smash-and-grab offences against parked cars in the Exhibition Road area. Be discreet with large amounts of cash, your belongings and travel documents; keep anything valuable in the hotel safe.

Road safety is definitely a major issue in Bahrain; with people from all over the world your best bet is to drive according to international traffic regulations, but expect to encounter aggressive habits from fellow road users. Make sure your insurance is valid and never drive without your licence on you.

Police

Police are divided into Public Security forces and Traffic Police. The Public Security officers wear pale green uniforms, while Traffic Police uniforms are white in the summer and light green and white in the winter. While the police are generally approachable, many of them speak no English. Call 999 in an emergency or 199 to report a traffic accident.

Physically Challenged Visitors

In general, facilities for people with disabilities are limited. Most of the larger hotels have wheelchair facilities, but make sure that they understand what you mean before booking. The malls and some supermarkets have designated special needs parking spaces, although other drivers tend to use them for the convenience.

Female Visitors

Women can visit Bahrain without any problem. The most you'll get is unwanted stares so if you don't want to draw attention to yourself, it's best to avoid wearing tight or revealing clothing, and walking in downtown Manama alone at night. In general, if you feel uncomfortable go to the nearest hotel or cafe.

Photography

Normal tourist photography is acceptable, but tourists should avoid photographing government and military buildings. When photographing locals, you should always ask for permission, particularly when wishing to take photos of women. There is a wide choice of film or memory cards available and processing is usually fast and relatively inexpensive. APS, 35mm and slide film can all be processed and most outlets will offer a computer so you can choose, edit and print photos from your digital camera on the spot.

Currency

Local currency is the Bahraini dinar (BD). One dinar is made up of 1,000 fils. Notes come in denominations of 500 fils, BD 1, BD 5, BD 10 and BD 20. Coin denominations are 5 fils, 10 fils, 25 fils, 50 fils and 100 fils, but in practice the 5 and 10 fils coins are hardly used. The dinar is pegged to the US dollar at a rate of US$1 to BD 0.377.

Banks & Money Exchanges

ATM machines are available in most malls and many major supermarket branches and the majority operate in both Arabic and English. Most ATMs will accept major cash and credit cards, Cirrus, Benefit and Plus. Some dispense cash in both dinars and US dollars. Opening hours vary, though most banks will have at least one branch that is open between 08:00 and 16:00 from Sunday to Thursday.

There are many money exchanges in Bahrain, particularly concentrated in Manama around the souk area and rates tend to be far more favourable than those given in the hotels. Money can also be exchanged in most banks and there are also unofficial independent money changers in the souk, these tend to be elderly men sitting on tin chairs at intersections and it is advisable to avoid using their services.

Electricity & Water

The electricity supply is 220 volts and 50 cycles and the socket type is the same as the three-point square plug British system. There are very few shortages for most of the year, with the exception of the hottest summer months, July and August, when the demand placed on the system by the increased use of air-conditioning units occasionally causes localised shortages for up to a few hours.

The mains tap water is desalinated and drinkable in the major residential areas, but is heavily chlorinated, so most people prefer to drink local and international brands of bottled water.

Telephone & Internet

There are no sim cards on offer to tourists on a short-term basis but with limited roaming capabilities it's worth taking along your passport and signing up for the pay-as-you-go option called SimSim. Batelco and MTC Vodaphone both have 24 hour airport branches and for around BD 8 (which includes BD 3 call or text credit) you can buy a sim card that can be topped up with widely available payment cards.

Phone boxes are available throughout Bahrain and take both coins and pre-paid cards that can be purchased in most shops. Calls using hotel lines can be expensive; up to twice the basic tariff.

Internet services are available in many internet cafes throughout Bahrain at a cost of about BD 1 per hour and many hotels also offer in-room internet facilities to guests. There is little, if any, censorship on internet sites. Local domain names in Bahrain end in .com.bh. Wi-Fi is increasingly popular and there are several cafes in Seef Mall (p.110) where you can surf the internet while slurping your coffee.

Lost & Found

If you have lost any property in Bahrain, the most useful thing to do, once you have spoken to the people employed in the place where you lost it and have left your contact details, is to hope for the best! As far as passports and travel documents are concerned, you should contact your own embassy or the airline (if it's a ticket) directly, and they'll tell you what to do. If an item has been stolen call 999 to report it to the police.

Annual Events & Public Holidays

Aside from religious holidays there are actually very few annual events in Bahrain. For one-offs, like conventions, football matches and concerts, read the newspapers and keep your eyes peeled for posters and flyers.

Various celebrations take place on National Day, including sporting, cultural and leisure activities. The day ends with an address by HH King Hamed at the National Stadium, accompanied by a massive fireworks display.

The Bahrain F1 Grand Prix is the highlight of the sporting calendar in Bahrain. It usually takes place in March or April and lasts three days. The Bahrain authorities relax visa requirements for the event and make every effort to ensure the success of the race, although trackside facilities still leave much to be desired. See www.bahraingp.com.bh for more details and dates for 2008.

Many of Bahrain's residents have been delighted by Spring of Culture. This new programme of dance, music, poetry and art is expected to run every year, running over several weeks in March and April. Visitors and residents can expect free admission to a variety of events but tickets are necessary for special performances at Arad Fort. For more information visit www.springofculture.com or call 3959 6748.

Public Holidays 2008

New Years Day	1 Jan
Islamic New Year	10 Jan
Ashoora - 2 days	19 Jan
Prophet's Birthday	20 Mar
Labour Day	1 May
Eid Al Fitr	2 Oct
Eid Al Adha	9 Dec
National Day	16 Dec
Islamic New Year	29 Dec

Arad Fort

Further Information

Get plugged into the media scene, learn how to send your auntie a postcard, say 'thank you' and know where to go when nature calls…

Newspapers & Magazines

There are two main English newspapers in Bahrain; the *Gulf Daily News* and the *Bahrain Tribune*, both of which are widely available and cost 200 fils. You can buy British papers and magazines at roughly double the UK retail price but many of the local magazines are worth a look. *Ooh La La*, *Bahrain Confidential* and *Bahrain This Month* all offer rounded views, listings and lifestyle news. There are also Middle Eastern versions of *Harper's Bazaar* and *Grazia* available which provide interesting insight into local fashions, nightlife and shopping.

Websites

While the design of many Bahrain websites left a lot to be desired in the past, things definitely are improving with sites such as www.bahrain.com – the new official portal for Bahrain, which is packed full of information on the country. Others worth checking out include www.bahrainthismonth.com with listings and events, while www.bahrainguide.org has some useful articles on life in the kingdom.

Postal Service

Bahrain's post system is rather old-fashioned and while it rarely loses mail, delays are common. It takes between three days and a week for a postcard to the UK, USA or Australia to arrive but letterboxes aren't particularly widespread so the easiest way to send something is to go directly to a post office. The largest post office is in the Diplomatic Area. With lots of courier companies competing for business it's best to shop around for the lowest prices and the same goes for shipping if you wish to send a large item home.

Public Toilets

There are no public toilets on the streets of Manama so your best bet is to dive into a mall or hotel lobby if you're caught short. Most toilets have attendants and generally you'll find both Arabic and western styles available.

Basic Arabic	
Yes	Na'am
No	La
Please	Min fadlak (m)/ Min fadliki (f)
Thank you	Shukran
God willing	In shaa'a l-aah
Greeting (Peace be upon you)	As-salaam alaykom
Hello	Marhaba
Hello (in reply)	Marhabteyn
Goodbye	Maa as-salaama
Goodbye (in reply)	Allah yisullmak
How are you?	Kayf haalak? (m) / Kayf haalik (f)
Fine, thank you	Al hamdu l-illah bikhair
Sorry	Aasif (m) / Aasifa (f)

Getting Around

You can enjoy getting around Manama on foot in the winter, but exploring the island by car or cab is your best bet.

With roadworks scattered throughout Manama and driving that could be filed under 'scary' you might find the roads a little daunting. Face the fear and do it anyway because the best way to see the whole island is on four wheels. Certain spots, like Adliya and the souk, are good for a wander but Bahrain simply isn't designed with pedestrians in mind. For a night out (especially at the weekend) simply grabbing a cab is ideal.

Bus

By far the cheapest way to get around, the buses are relatively new and air conditioned and are clearly marked on the front and side with their destinations. A ticket will cost only a few hundred fils, payable in cash (there are no prepaid passes available) and buses are reasonably frequent. However, there is no easy access to bus timetables, which means catching one is a bit of a hit-and-miss affair.

Car

Driving is on the right-hand side of the road and the majority of the cars are automatic which makes sense for driving in the city. The road system is fairly well developed, but recent years have seen a surge in the number of cars owned and this has led to increasing pressure on the country's roads. The country is so small that even a 'long' journey with a traffic jam doesn't usually exceed 30 minutes. In the centre of Manama the roads are older and are limited to one or two lanes.

Blue signs indicate the main areas within the country and brown signs show heritage or tourism sites, and other places of interest. Roads are also named on smaller blue signs and these are often either numbers or names of prominent people in the country's recent history. However, most people don't refer to the roads by their official names, and in fact, with a few exceptions, probably don't even know what they are officially called. People refer to the roads primarily by landmarks they pass, so instead of being told, 'go down Khalifa Road', you could quite easily be told 'it's in Adliya, behind the Ferrari showroom'.

While the road infrastructure meets international standards, the general standard of driving does not. Although driving is perhaps of a higher standard than many of the neighbouring countries, there are nonetheless regular accidents so wearing your seatbelt is highly recommended

Car Rental Agencies

Avis	1753 1144
Bahrain Car Hiring Co.	1753 4343
Budget	1753 4100
Elite Rent-A-Car	1731 1883
Europcar	1769 2999
Express Rent-A-Car	1753 2525
Hanco Rent-A-Car	1731 0656
Hertz	1732 1358
National Car Rental	1731 1169
Thrifty	1773 5991

(and now required by law for all passengers in the front). Drivers are often somewhat self-centred, lacking lane and speed discipline. People also regularly use mobile phones when driving, which reduces their awareness (although a law has been recently been brought in making this illegal). There are lots of car hire companies present in the arrivals hall at the airport so don't settle for the first quoted price.

Taxi

Taxis are metered and are easily identified by orange panels on the front and rear wings (1726 6266). Taxis to and from the airport are subject to a BD 1 surcharge. A ride from the airport to Manama should cost in the region of BD 3. A journey within Manama should not run to more than BD 2.

Walking

It is safe and enjoyable to stroll around the old Manama Souk. The whole area is a maze of small roads and alleys, ideally suited to exploring on foot, although it can be unpleasantly hot and sticky during the summer months. Another nice stroll is along the Corniche.

> **Dodgy Taxis**
>
> **Don't be fooled by a taxi driver claiming not to have a meter; all taxis have them fitted by law. However, they will often try to get a higher fare by pretending not to have a meter (check behind the tissue box by the gear lever), or that it is in fact broken. If they refuse to use it, don't be afraid to get out and find another, more honest, taxi driver.**

King Fahad Causeway

Places To Stay

From luxurious desert spas to homely apartments to make you feel like a local, Bahrain has everything under the Arabian sun.

Bahrain's target tourist market is in the middle to upper range and is well supplied with hotels and serviced apartments. There are over 80 hotels in the Manama area with over 7,000 rooms available. All hotels and apartments are generally up to international standards; although visitors from the developed world might be inclined to knock a few stars off the 2 and 3 star places.

A cheaper alternative to booking into a hotel, particularly if you are staying for more than a week, is to rent furnished apartments. The apartments come fully furnished, including household appliances and linen, and can also provide maid services. Serviced apartments from top-class hotels include Gulf Executive Residence (1772 6178, www.gulfhotelbahrain.com) which have excellent facilities, or you can book with a company like Elite (1782 2999, www.eliteapartments.net) who have apartments all over the kingdom.

There are three youth hostels in Bahrain run by Bahrain Youth Hostel Society (www.byhs.org.bh) including the main one in Al Juffair (1772 7170) and one in Seef (1755 6962). All provide beds and washing facilities only and cost around BD 7.500 for a single room with bath and BD 4.500 per person sharing for a double room with bath.

The Ritz-Carlton, Bahrain Hotel & Spa

Al Bander Hotel & Resort
1770 1201
Nxt Bahrain Yacht Club, Sitra   www.albander.com
Located at the southern end of Sitra, this resort has a wide
range of facilities including swimming pools and watersports
at their private beach. Rooms are either cabana style or in
chalets and there are activities for kids and a variety of food
and dining options. Map 1-D4

Banyan Tree Desert Spa & Resort
1784 5000
Nr Al Areen Wildlife Park   www.banyantree.com/bahrain
This all-villa resort is located close to the F1 International Circuit
and offers a truly luxurious hideaway. With the Middle East's
most extensive spa, outstanding restaurants and conference
facilites, this is the perfect place for both work and play. Map 1-C5

Crowne Plaza
1753 1122
Al Fatih Highway, Diplomatic Area   www.ichotelsgroup.com
Located in the Diplomatic Area it has 246 rooms including 10
standard suites and two royal suites. Facilities include an outdoor
swimming pool, two gymnasiums, a beauty salon, restaurants,
coffee shops, a nightclub and a business centre. Map 2-G1

Diplomat Radisson SAS Hotel
1753 1666
Al Fatih Highway, Diplomatic Area   www.radissonsas.com
Centrally located in the heart of Manama, this hotel has 226
rooms and 20 suites. Facilities include an outdoor swimming
pool, a beauty salon and a good selection of popular
restaurants and bars. The business centre offers 10 meeting
and conference halls. Map 2-G2

Golden Tulip Bahrain
1753 3000
Palace Ave, Diplomatic Area   www.goldentulipbahrain.com
Located in the city centre, the Golden Tulip has 250 rooms
including eight suites. It has several restaurants, lounge
bars, coffee shops and a ballroom. It also has a fully serviced
business and communications centre. Map 2-G2

Gulf Hotel
1771 3000
Off Al Fatih Highway, Adliya   www.gulfhotelbahrain.com
Just a five-minute drive from the city centre, the Gulf Hotel has
352 rooms including eight suites. Its facilities include an outdoor
swimming pool and shops. It has several restaurants and bars
that offer some of the best eating out in Bahrain. Map 2-H4

Mercure Grand Hotel
1758 4400
Off Shk Khalifa Bin Salman Highway   www.mercurebahrain.com
Situated close to the main malls in Seef, the Mercure offers
some fantastic dining options as well as a rooftop pool. There
are 72 senior suites, 48 family suites and one penthouse as
well as two meeting rooms. Map 2-C2

Mövenpick
1746 0000
Nr Airport, Muharraq   www.moevenpick-hotels.com
Located next to the airport, it has 106 rooms including
10 suites and eight luxury suites. Facilities include
restaurants, a bar, a coffee shop, shops, a ballroom, a pool,
a gymnasium, a beauty salon and babysitting services. It
also has a fully serviced business centre and six conference/
meeting rooms. Map 1-D1

Novotel Al Dana Resort
1729 8008

Off Shk Hamad Causeway   www.novotel-bahrain.com

The Novotel is an attractive resort conveniently located on the causeway just minutes from the airport. Equipped with 172 rooms, there are extensive fitness and recreation facilities including a gym and a private beach. There is also a host of dining and entertainment options. Map 2-H1

Regency InterContinental
1722 7777

King Faisal Hwy, City Centre   www.ichotelsgroup.com

Situated in the City Centre, this hotel is a great choice for business travellers. Facilities include a swimming pool, 24 hour gym, gift shops, bars and restaurants, in addition to a choice of meeting rooms. Conference equipment can be hired. Map 3-A1

The Ritz-Carlton, Bahrain Hotel & Spa
1758 0000

Off King Abdulla Avenue, Seef   www.ritzcarlton.com

Situated on the seafront in Seef, just 10 minutes drive from the city centre, it has a large expanse of private beach and its own marina. With 264 rooms including 22 suites and villas on its 20 acre site, it also boasts nine quality restaurants, the luxurious Ritz-Carlton Spa and comprehensive business facilities. Map 2-C1

Sheraton Bahrain Hotel
1753 3533

King Faisal Hwy, Diplomatic Area   www.starwoodhotels.com

The Sheraton is near the Diplomatic Area and has 260 rooms. Facilities include several restaurants and lounge bars, an outdoor swimming pool, a health club, two ballrooms, four meeting rooms and three boardrooms. Map 2-G2

Novotel Al Dana Resort

Exploring

Exploring Bahrain

Beyond the hotels and villas lies a world of adventure, tradition and excitement. So where do you want to go first?

Amid the dramatic new architecture, city sights, open space and luxury villas, is a place where you will find a warm welcome. Bahrain is often overlooked in favour of its more vibrant and attention-seeking Gulf neighbours but it has a lot to offer visitors. From the souks, malls and high rises of metropolitan Manama to the deserted shores of the Hawar Islands, the kingdom is full of opportunities to experience Middle Eastern culture, both old and new.

With a rich history and inspiring future, Bahrain is an exciting choice for a visit; still known as the island of golden smiles, the people are warm, friendly and welcoming. Although the tourism infrastructure is still in its infancy, progress is being made at an impressive rate and this chapter will guide you through the different areas of the island, from the cosmopolitan capital to the desert plains. You'll find the main attractions, sights and landmarks for each district, as well the best choices for dining, drinking and entertainment to point you in the right direction; each destination is clearly marked on the easy-to-use map at the beginning of each section.

Over the following pages we have divided up Bahrain into the main areas to make life a bit easier and allowing you to plan your trip in the most effective way. There is a quick directory for visitors and you'll get an idea of what there is to see and do – beach clubs, malls, spas, galleries, museums, islands and activities are all on offer, and if you're short on time, you can always take a tour. The capital city of Manama has been split into three – centre, east and west – for easy navigation and the other parts of the kingdom have been simplified. The north-west, central and southern areas and Muharraq are all away from Manama and you'll find map references for every recommendation to help you find your way to the many diverse attractions.

Take advantage of Bahrain's unique landscape and get away from the city sights with a trip to the desert, or to truly escape, book some quality time at one of the island's luxury hotel spas. Get the adrenaline pumping at the Formula One International Circuit or jet off on a speed boat to explore the other islands and maybe see some dolphins on the way.

Whether this is your first time to the Middle East or you just wish to see another side to this fascinating part of the world, this section will help you explore everything this kingdom has to offer.

Outside Bahrain

The other countries of the Gulf Cooperation Council (GCC) are also worth a visit, especially if you want to get a fuller picture of the traditions and culture of the Middle East. Whether you want to go driving in Oman's magnificent mountains, hit the shops and the bars in Dubai or experience Kuwait's colourful heritage, each country is just a short, cheap flight from Bahrain.

At A Glance

Forts, beaches, spas and culture can all be yours, if you know where to look.

Bahrain is a relatively small kingdom, but there's lots packed in and loads to do. Below you'll find attractions and activities organised according to type, so you can fill your days with fun and still have time to spare.

Heritage Sites

Museums & Art Galleries

The Painted Village

Manama City Centre

At the heart of the action, Manama's city centre offers modern hotels and unexpected heritage spots in a charming juxtaposition.

The Financial Harbour is changing the face of the capital forever and the impressive architecture dominates the Bahrain skyline. In the city centre you'll find most of the hotels, as well as museums, embassies, government offices and high-rise office buildings and as a result of all this action, the roads can be very congested. Many fine dining options can be found in the hotels but for more low-key menu choices, seek out the shawarma and juice kiosks dotted among the skyscrapers.

Take some time out and learn more about Bahrain's background; the beautiful but well-hidden Currency Museum (p.42) is in the Diplomatic Area and for more ideas go to Bab Al Bahrain (p.42), a building that was previously government offices but now houses the Tourist Information Office.

With excellent restaurants in the hotels come outstanding brunch options (the Diplomat Radisson SAS is a favourite with expats) and some great nights out, in fact, most of the bars, pubs and nightclubs in the main hotels are all worth a try.

There aren't many shopping malls around here but the Sheraton Complex, behind the Sheraton Hotel, is handy for designer threads. For less genuine items head to the souk where you'll find high quality gold alongside fabric, souvenirs and spices. For a truly special present browse Gold City (p.115) for pearls. After all that shopping the little

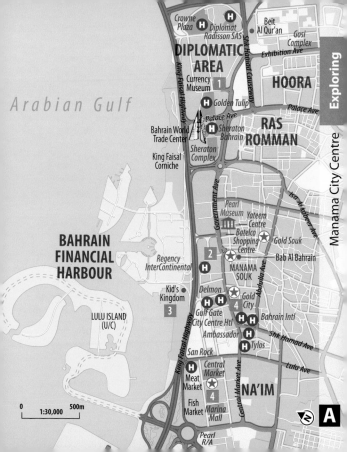

Arabian Gulf

Crowne Plaza

Diplomat
Radisson SAS

Beit
Al Qur'an

Gosi
Complex

Exhibition Ave

DIPLOMATIC
AREA

HOORA

King Faisal Highway

Currency
Museum

1

Golden Tulip

Palace Ave

Palace Ave

RAS
ROMMAN

Bahrain World
Trade Center

Sheraton
Bahrain

Sheraton
Complex

King Faisal
Corniche

Government Ave

Pearl
Museum

Yateem
Centre

Batelco
Shopping
Centre

Gold Souk

Bab Al Bahrain

Isa Al Kabeer Ave

BAHRAIN
FINANCIAL
HARBOUR

Regency
InterContinental

2

MANAMA
SOUK

Kid's
Kingdom

3

Delmon

Gold
City

4

Abdulla Ave

LULU ISLAND
(U/C)

Gulf Gate
City Centre Htl

Bahrain Intl

Ambassador

Shk Hamad Ave

Tylos

San Rock

King Faisal Highway

Central
Market

Meat
Market

NA'IM

Central Market Ave

Lulu Ave

Fish
Market

Marina
Mall

0   500m
1:30,000

Pearl
R/A

A

ones might deserve a treat and Kid's Kingdom (below) is just the place.

For **restaurants and bars** in the area, see p.126

Bab Al Bahrain   1721 1595
Opp Post Office, Government Road, Manama

Originally built in 1945, Bab Al Bahrain translates as Gateway of Bahrain and was then right on the waterfront; traders used to tie their dhows up on the jetty outside before taking their goods to the souk. These days, the only traders around are in the nearby Financial Harbour. It was extensively renovated in the late 1980s and now is home to the Tourist Information Office and a shop that sells local handicrafts, guidebooks, maps and postcards. Map A 2

Currency Museum   1753 5535
Bahrain Monetary Agency Building, Manama

Sadly, this little museum is often overlooked and even staff in the building seem unaware of its existence and there isn't even a car park. Situated on the first floor of the Bahrain Monetary Agency, there are exhibitions on rare coins and banknotes so you'll learn the history of what you're spending. You will have to hand over some form of identification to gain entry and it's worth calling ahead to check opening times. Map A 1

Kid's Kingdom   1722 7476
King Faisal Corniche, Manama

With bungee bouncers, a bouncy castle, giant inflatable slide and late opening hours children can tire themselves out while you admire the view of the nearby docked dhows. Entry is free with a charge for each ride. Map A **3**

Manama Souk, Gold City & Central Market
Nr Pearl Roundabout, Manama

All your shopping needs are catered for here, from fresh fish to fake designer handbags. Get up early and witness the organised chaos of Central Market (see p.115 in the Shopping section) or barter down the price of some jewellery in Gold City (p.115); a dazzling display of bling in 152 shops. Manama Souk (p.115) behind Gold City is a confusing maze of covered alleyways where you'll find food, fabric, shoes, souvenirs, more gold, and almost anything else you could imagine. It really does provide sensory overload with enthusiastic bargaining, spicy smells and crammed streets. Just remember which entrance you came in and don't get too lost! Map A **4**

Going Up...

In this area you'll see a lot of construction work as the dramatic towers of Bahrain World Trade Center and the new skyscrapers of the Financial Harbour are finished. They are particularly useful landmarks for navigating around Manama if you're lost or trying to find a main road out of the city; just look to the sky, head in their direction and you can't go wrong.

If you only do one thing in...

Manama City Centre

Stroll past the Bahrain World Trade Center and strain your neck looking up at the giant wind turbines.

Best for...

Eating & Drinking: Upmarket Far Eastern cuisine at Kontiki Asia (p.128) at The Diplomat Radisson SAS Hotel, then Harvesters pub (p.132) at the Crowne Plaza for live music and deals on drinks.

Sightseeing: You can't miss the Pearl Roundabout, but you'll see the real Bahrain in the tiny streets of the Manama Souk (p.115).

Shopping: Glittering, multi-storey Gold City (p.115) for antiques, pearls, pashminas and, of course, gold.

Families: Kid's Kingdom (p.42) or the jungle-themed foodcourt at Marina Mall (p.110).

Clockwise from top left: Gold City, Financial Harbour, Bab Al Bahrain

Manama City East

Here you will find most of Bahrain's nightlife and many cultural attractions, but pretty busy traffic.

This area has some of the finest attractions, including Bahrain National Museum (p.48) with its intriguing exhibits, several art galleries and The Children & Youth Science Centre (p.53).

Adliya offers sophisticated dining experiences, with dozens of restaurants serving food from all over the world as well some excellent shawarmas and shisha cafes. See page 134 in the Going Out chapter for venues. There is also a wealth of oriental carpet and antique jewellery shops where you can work up an appetite haggling over a truly special souvenir.

Hoora's Exhibition Avenue (p.112) was once a single lane road but has burgeoned into a major hotel, entertainment and shopping area, which unfortunately isn't very safe at night, but is an excellent spot for buying cheap technology, fast food and getting a taste of a district that's a bit rough around the edges.

On the corniche, opposite the dramatic off-shore fountain, is Funland (p.50). Here, you can ice-skate and bowl or let the kids try their luck in the video arcade while you relax with a coffee. If you're up for some outdoor action, the Marina Club (p.52) is a good spot to take a jetski out and boat cruises leave from Island Tours (p.51) next door and the Novotel Al Dana Resort (p.52) nearby.

For **restaurants and bars** in the area, see p.134

Arabian Gulf

BAHRAIN
FINANCIAL
HARBOUR

King Faisal Corniche

Crowne Plaza

Diplomat Radisson SAS

Shk Hamad Causeway

Novotel Al Dana Resort **5**

King Faisal Hwy

Bahrain National Museum

3

Art Centre

King Faisal Corniche

King Faisal Hwy

DIPLOMATIC AREA

Beit Al Qur'an

4

Bahrain Phoenicia

Al Fatih Hwy

Marina Club

6

Gulf Gate

Regency InterContinental

King Faisal Hwy

Government Ave

CITY CENTRE

Bab Al Bahrain

Abdulla Ave

Bahrain World Trade Center

Sheraton Bahrain

RAS ROMMAN

2

La Fontaine Centre of Contemporary Art

Palace Ave

Metropolitan

Baisan Tower

Funland Centre

9

Baisan Intl

Marina Corniche

HOORA

Zubara Ave

Manama Tower

MAKHARQAH

A'IM

ZARARIE
Modern Craft Centre
Shk Mohd Ave

Shk Isa al Kabeer Ave

Shk Hamad Ave

Shk Abdulla Ave

Shk Mohd Ave

Al Muharraq Ave

Gudaibiyah Ave

Exhibition Ave

UFOOL

Water Garden

SALMANIYA

Andalus Garden

Salmaniya Garden

Shk Daij Ave

QUDAYBIYAH

Al Fateh Grand Mosque

Riviera

Al Safir

Shk Isa al Kabeer Ave

Shk Salman Hwy

Salmaniya Ave

Salmaniya Ave

Old Palace
Al Bustan

Qudaybiyah Palace

Al Fateh Islamic Centre

Awal Ave

Al Fatih Hwy

Exhibition Ave

ADLIYA

Ramada

Gulf Hotel

Gulf Intl Convention Centre

NJ

SUQAYA

Oman Ave

Oman Ave

Al Osra Ave

Naseem Ave

Juffair Sports Hall

Juffair International

Elite

Shk Isa Ave

Al Adliya Ave

Shk Isa Ave

JUFFAIR

ABU ASHIRAH

Al Jazira

Al Qudaybiya Ave

ABU GAZAL

Shk Isa Ave

MAHOOZ

8

Children & Youth Science Centre

Mahooz Ave

QURAIFA

Umm Al Hassam Ave

Shk Isa Bin Salman Hwy

ADHARI

0   1km

1:45,000

1

Arabesque Art Gallery

UMM AL HASSAM

N

B

Arabesque Art Gallery

Off Umm al Hassam Avenue,
Umm al Hassam

1772 2916
www.arabesque-gal.org

Located in Umm al Hassam, the gallery offers a huge array of
paintings with many by one of Bahrain's best known artists,
Abdul Wahab Al Koheji. This is also the place to find hand-
produced silkscreens, antique Middle Eastern maps and art
including Victorian engravings. If you're just looking, there are
regular exhibitions by visiting artists or if you want to try out
your own talents, try one of the popular art classes. Map B **1**

Bahrain National Museum

Al Fatih Highway, Hoora

1729 2977
www.bnmuseum.com

Situated at the top of the corniche near the causeway
to Muharraq, the museum is housed in a series of low
buildings and has a large car park. Get a guidebook from
the museum shop and start exploring; there are exhibits
on natural history and life before oil and air conditioning
transformed the kingdom as well as the thrilling Hall of
Graves which children will love. The museum has enjoyed
visiting collections recently with the Pharaoh exhibition
including the treasures of Tutankhamun. Entrance is 500 fils
for adults and children are admitted free of charge. Map B **3**

Beit Al Qur'an

Nr Diplomat Radisson SAS Hotel,
Diplomatic Area

1729 0101
www.beitalquran.com

Located near the Sheikh Hamad Causeway, this modern
building is somewhat ugly, but on closer inspection you

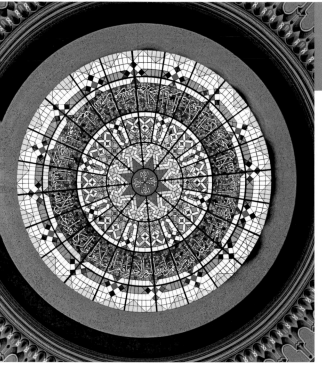

can see the effort taken to engrave the walls with Arabic calligraphy. Beit Al Qu'ran translates to House of the Quran, and it displays rare Islamic manuscripts and artwork including beautiful examples with intricate calligraphy and geometric designs. Entrance is free but donations are welcome and all visitors should dress conservatively. Map B 4

Funland
1729 2313
Off Al Fatih Highway, Hoora   www.funlandcentre.com

Funland on the Marina Corniche has a bowling alley with 18 lanes and a full-size ice-skating rink. The centre is open for bowling from 09:00 to 01:00 and for skating from 09:00 to 23:30. The prices are BD 2.500 for two hours of ice skating, which includes hire of skates. There is a concession of BD 2 per person for a group of 10 or more people, but you need to book in advance. Bowling costs BD 1 per game from Saturday to Wednesday and BD 1.600 per game on Thursday and Friday. Kids can refuel and adults can take escape for a break at the coffee shop. Map B 9

Gulf Discovery
3648 6428
Novotel Al Dana Resort, Shk Hamad Causeway

Gulf Discovery offer dhow cruises from the Novotel Al Dana Resort on request, leaving at 09:15 and returning at 17:00, costing BD 20 for adults and BD 15 for children. The star of their fleet is the recently converted 60 foot 'Scaramouch', which can accommodate 25 passengers. Tours are tailored to customers' preferences and they offer charters for everything from sunset cruises scuba diving, fishing and dolphin watching to excursions to places such as Jaradah Island. Map B 5

Island Tours
1729 4439

Nxt Marina Club, Al Fatih Highway, Hoora

Situated next to the Marina Club, this tour company offers a range of packages and trips, from a few hours on a speed boat spotting dolphins to dinner cruises and trips to the deserted tidal sand bar island of Jaradah. The lunch cruises depart on a 52 foot yacht at 12:00, travel through the waves for about an hour and eventually dock on Jaradah. The crew will prepare a buffet-style lunch while you explore the shallow waters from the yacht's swim platform or venture out into deeper water on a jetski. After a two hour sojourn, the trip back to shore often includes a little dolphin watching too. The lunch cruise arrives back at 16:00 and costs BD 25 for adults and BD 15 for kids. For more on their boat trips see p.89 and p.90. Map B 6

La Fontaine Centre of Contemporary Art
1723 0123

92 Hoora Avenue, Hoora   www.lafontainecentre.com

This place is a true architectural gem and an unexpected find in hectic Hoora. The wind towers, cool corridors, a Pilates studio that has to be seen to be believed, world-class restaurant, extensive spa (see p.102), regular film screenings and art exhibitions make La Fontaine a unique jewel in Bahrain's crown. The enormous fountain in the courtyard is alone worth a visit, but you'll find so much more. Map B 2

Marina Club

1729 1527
Off Al Fatih Highway, Hoora www.marinaclub.info

Popular with families, the Marina Club has a large, partially covered swimming pool, a kid's pool with slide and plenty of room for running around. There are also squash and tennis courts and a beach where you can rent jetskis or play volleyball. If catching some rays is more your thing then take advantage of the pool-side menu and enjoy generous sandwiches, fresh juices and waiter-service in the sun. Non-members can use the outdoor pool and beach from 08:00 for BD 1 per visit and there is plenty of parking outside which is free if using the facilities. Keep an eye out for special events here too – Bahrain-based and international DJs have played some fantastic outdoor sets in recent months, including the region's first ever full moon party, national celebrations and the after-party for the Formula One Grand Prix celebrations in 2007. Map B 6

Novotel Al Dana Resort

1729 8008
Off Shk Hamad Causeway www.novotel-bahrain.com

There is a real holiday feel to this hotel complex, with a large lagoon-style swimming pool, health club, lots of sun loungers, swim-up bar, pool-side dining and shisha and even a small beach with bar, boat trips and watersports. The food is excellent, with barbecue buffets from Mediterranean restaurant Zytoun (p.149) and La Perle (p.143) for French cuisine on site. Kids are also well looked after with a dedicated play area complete with helpers and regular activities – ring for the schedule. Map B 5

The Children & Youth Science Centre   1772 1132
Nr Kuwait Avenue, Umm al Hassam

This hands-on museum for information-hungry youngsters is located in Umm al Hassam and boasts plenty of fun, colourful exhibits. With friendly, helpful staff and no entrance fee, this science centre is the perfect place to inspire a little learning in your little ones. Map B **6**

The Water Garden
Shk Salman Highway, Ghufool

The oldest park in Bahrain is the Water Garden, which is located in the Ghufool District off Sheikh Salman Highway. This park is very popular with local families, but it does not have a swimming pool. There is a big lake, kiosks selling ice cream, popcorn and toys, and several sideshows for children, such as swings, roundabouts, bumper cars, a swing boat and a train that runs around the lake. Most of the sideshows cost around 400 or 500 fils a go. Entrance is 500 fils and you can hire a pedal boat for BD 1. Unfortunately, the upkeep of this park is not always that great and at times you may find the toilets are dirty and see rubbish floating in the lake. Map B **7**

Big Fun For Little Ones

When it's too hot to explore the desert, the huge shopping malls offer fun and varied activities with mini rollercoasters, arcades, mazes, ball pools and slides. You'll also find children well catered for at restaurants, with special menus, high-chairs, baby-sitting services, summer camps and regular events at some of the larger hotels on the island.

a work of art is a love letter to the world

charlie chaplin

If you only do one thing in...

Manama City East

Take your time choosing a spot for dinner in Adliya then watch the world and supercharged cars cruise by.

Best for...

Eating & Drinking: Take a walk around Adliya and choose from the dozens of restaurants (p.134) and, if the mood takes you, head to BJs (p.151); arguably the best club in Bahrain.

Sightseeing: Bahrain National Museum (p.48) showcases some insightful exhibits and the on-site shop has some great souvenirs.

Shopping: Head to 'Carpet Street' in Adliya to do some haggling over homewares or Exhibition Avenue (p.112) for cheap electronics.

Relaxation: A massage at La Fontaine (p.102) is hard to beat or for more Arabian relaxation, smoke some shisha in one of the many nearby cafes.

Families: Take a trip to the science centre for some hands-on learning or be bowled over by Funland (p.50).

Clockwise from top: Bahrain National Museum, Manama skyline, La Fontaine Centre of Contemporary Art

Manama City West

If you've come to Bahrain to hit the shops then head to Seef, and for some local history, the island's oldest mosque is here too.

Built entirely on reclaimed land, this relatively new part of town is a retail retreat with several large malls including Seef Mall (p.110), Al Aali Shopping Complex (p.108), Dana Mall (p.110) and Bahrain Mall (p.108) as well as some exclusive boutiques hidden away in the high quality hotels. If flexing the plastic doesn't appeal or there are kids to entertain, the malls also offer respite from the heat in the form of multiplex cinemas and dedicated play zones. Al Khamis Mosque (below), is worth a visit and is a refreshing change from the shiny shops.

For fine dining you'll find some excellent options in the hotels or for simple foodcourt fodder there are loads of choice from international big names to local cuisine cafes – just wander around and see what takes your fancy.

Providing the weather is kind, head to Al Qassari Water Park (p.58) or the beach at the Ritz-Carlton (p.59) then finish off the day with sundowners at Trader Vic's (p.154). It's a tough life in the Gulf!

*For **restaurants and bars** in the area, see p.152*

Al Khamis Mosque
Off Shk Salman Highway, Manama

This mosque is the oldest in Bahrain and is thought to have been built 1,300 years ago by the Ummayed Caliph Omar bin Abdul

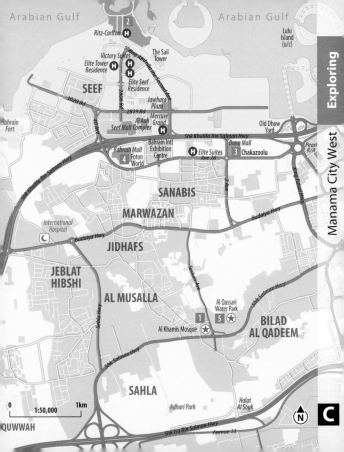

Arabian Gulf

Arabian Gulf

Lulu
Island
(u/c)

2 H
Ritz-Carlton

Victory Suites H
Elite Tower H
Residence H
Elite Seef H
Residence

The Sail
Tower

SEEF

3020 Rd

40 Ave

2819 Rd
Al Aali
Seef Mall Complex

Jawhara
Plaza

Mercure
Grand

Shk Khalifa Bin Salman Hwy

Old Dhow
Yard

Bahrain
Fort

Bahrain Intl
Exhibition
Centre

Bahrain Mall
Foton
World **4**

H Elite Suites
Ave 28

Dana Mall
3 Chakazoolu

2 Ave

Pearl
R/A

King Faisal Hwy

Manama City West

Shk Khalifa Bin Salman Hwy

SANABIS

MARWAZAN

International
Hospital C

Budaiya Hwy

Budaiya Hwy

JIDHAFS

**JEBLAT
HIBSHI**

Shk Isa Hwy

AL MUSALLA

Jaafari Ave

Shk Salman Hwy

Al Qassari
Water Park

1 Al Khamis Mosque ★

5 ★

**BILAD
AL QADEEM**

Shk Salman Hwy

SAHLA

Adhari Park

Halat
Al Souk

0   1km
1:50,000

QUWWAH

Shk Isa Bin Salman Hwy

Avenue 13

N

C

Aziz. The two minarets were added later, one during the 12th century and the other in the 16th century. The site is well looked after, but there is no information available, or any other facilities, including toilets. The mosque, which is located beside Sheikh Salman Highway, opposite Khamis Police Station, has been extensively renovated with one of the minarets being taken down and rebuilt completely a few years ago. Map C **1**

Al Qassari Water Park   1740 0739
Nr Al Khamis Mosque, Jidhafs

Al Qassari Water Park reopened after being partly destroyed by fire during the mid 90s. It is located off Sheikh Salman Highway, on the bend just before you reach the traffic lights at Al Khamis Mosque. There are three swimming pools, a large one for adults and two smaller ones for children. Attendants are on duty at each pool and it is possible to arrange swimming lessons. The shower blocks and toilets are clean. Ladies do not generally go into the water, but tend to sit around the children's pools. Icecream, cold drinks and sandwiches are on sale. The entry fee is BD 1 for a two-hour session. There are five sessions throughout the day from 10:00 to 12:00, 13:00 to 15:00, 15:00 to 17:00, 17:30 to 19:30 and 20:00 to 22:00. Phone for further details. Map C **5**

Chakazoolu   1755 8500
Dana Mall, Sanabis

In Dana Mall (p.110) you'll find this indoor theme park on two floors with rides, bumper cars, a rollercoaster, games and places to buy food. Entry is free, but you need to buy a rechargeable card (minimum charge BD 2) to use the games and rides. If you buy a card for BD 5, you get another BD 2 free. Video games cost 250 fils a go. Map C 3

Foton World
1755 6112
Nxt Bahrain Mall, Seef

Next door to Bahrain Mall (p.108) is Foton World, an indoor theme park that has small boat rides, bumper cars, a roller coaster, games and food outlets. Entry is free and children can enter alone and remain unattended, allowing you to explore and shop. Games and rides cost 400 to 500 fils, so it's a fun and cheap way to fill an afternoon, out of the summer sun. Map C 4

The Ritz-Carlton, Bahrain Hotel & Spa
1758 0000
Off King Abdulla the Second Ave, Seef   www.ritzcarlton.com

As one of the leading hotels in Bahrain, if you're not lucky enough to be staying, you really should visit. There is a great range of restaurants and bars or try the afternoon tea for something a bit special. The pool and beach are superb, as are the spa facilities which are open to non-guests – and are conveniently located next to some very exclusive shops to catch you off-guard after a massage! The Burlington Club (p.157) is a cigar bar with an exclusive feel, perfect for a drink before dinner at one of the restaurants. Trader Vic's (p.154) is at the side of the hotel and the outdoor area is especially popular – try one of the cocktails and Asian-inspired nibbles while listening to the live band. You'll really feel like you're away from it all. Map C 2

If you only do one thing in...

Manama City West

Enjoy the pleasures of shopping, dining and movie-watching all under Bahrain's biggest roof at Seef Mall.

Best for...

Eating & Drinking: Try the international cuisine at Neyran at the Mercure Grand Hotel (p.152) then cocktails by the water courtesy of Trader Vic's at the Ritz-Carlton (p.154).

Sightseeing: Seef Mall (p.110), Bahrain's largest shopping centre is a major attraction or for some authentic culture visit Al Khamis Mosque (p.56).

Shopping: Spend the day mall hopping; they are remarkably close together and all offer a different shopping experience.

Relaxation: The spa at the Ritz-Carlton (p.102) is unrivalled with an extensive treatment menu and high quality products.

Families: Kids will love the indoor theme parks or head to the luxurious cinema at Dana Mall (p.110). for some icecream and quiet time.

Seef Mall

North-West Bahrain

Pottery, forts and burial mounds – this might be where the expats live but there was a lot happening before they arrived...

There are some outstanding cultural attractions and sights here; Bahrain Fort (below), offers great views and the nearby 'painted village' of Karbabad is a worth a look too. Keep an eye out for roadside burial mounds, pick up some local pottery along Budaiya Highway, get some history at Saar Settlement (p.65) or Barbar Temple (p.64) then stop off for coffee at one of the many cafes. The short drive out of Manama will show you where many of Bahrain's resident expats call home and offers a different insight to this diverse and fascinating community.
For *restaurants and bars* in the area, see p.158

Bahrain Fort
Off Shk Khalifa Bin Salman Highway, Nr Karbabad Village
The site of the first professional archaeological dig in Bahrain in 1953, this impressive 16th century Portuguese fort is built on the remains of several previous settlements, going back to the Dilmun era around 2800BC. There are several large, informative notices dotted around the area, and some information booklets are available in English. Entry is free and the fort is open from 08:00 to 20:00 every day including Friday. Follow the signs to Karbabad Village. The small village at the entrance to the fort is remarkable in that the houses

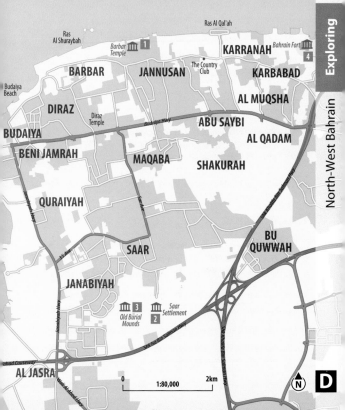

A r a b i a n   G u l f

Ras Al Qal'ah

Ras Al Shuraybah

Barbar Temple **1**

KARRANAH

Bahrain Fort **4**

The Country Club

BARBAR

JANNUSAN

KARBABAD

Budaiya Beach

DIRAZ

Diraz Temple

AL MUQSHA

Budaiya Hwy

ABU SAYBI

BUDAIYA

BENI JAMRAH

MAQABA

AL QADAM

Sitra Ave

SHAKURAH

QURAIYAH

35 Ave

BU QUWWAH

SAAR

JANABIYAH

Old Burial Mounds **3**

Saar Settlement **2**

Janabiyah Hwy

Shk Isa Bin Salman Hwy

Shk Khalifa Bin Salman Hwy

Shk Isa Bin Salman Hwy

ahad Causeway

AL JASRA

Wali Al Ahad Hwy

0   1:80,000   2km

N

D

are covered in brightly coloured murals. Every inch of space, including the water tanks on the roofs, the TV dish aerials and the air-conditioning units, have been painted. Well worth a photo or two! Map D 4

Barbar Temple
Off Budaiya Highway, Nr Barbar Village

Barbar Temple, which was excavated in the 1950s and 60s, dates back to around 2200BC. The remains are remarkable in that the structures are made of large stone blocks fitted together without plaster. Many objects retrieved from the site can be seen in the Bahrain National Museum. Barbar Temple is surrounded by a wire fence and guarded by a soldier – but don't let that put you off! There are two noticeboards giving general information in English and Arabic at the entrance to the site and the temple is well signposted from Budaiya Highway. Map D 1

The Burial Mounds
South of Saar Village & West of A'ali Village

One of the most remarkable sights in Bahrain is the vast area of burial mounds at Saar, near A'ali Village, at Hamad Town and at Sakhir. The mounds were built during the Dilmun, Tylos and Helenistic periods and are anything from two to four thousand years old. The largest burial mounds, which are known as the Royal Tombs, are found in and around A'ali Village, where the traditional pottery kilns are located. The mounds originally extended all the way from Saar down to Zallaq, but thousands of them have been destroyed to make way for new roads and houses. Map D 3

Bahrain Fort

Saar Settlement
South of Saar Village

It is advisable to visit this major archaeological site, south of the present-day Saar Village, during the winter months from January to April, when a team of British archaeologists usually arrives in Bahrain to work on the site. The settlement dates from 2000BC and you can see the remains of many small houses built on either side of the main road which leads up to the temple. The site is not signposted, though it appears on some maps as Ancient Saar. Map D 2

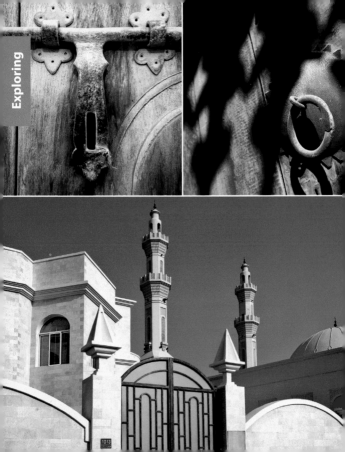

If you only do one thing in...

North-West Bahrain

Be a culture vulture at some of the kingdom's
most important heritage sites. And don't forget
your camera.

Best for...

Eating & Drinking: Cappucino Café (see p.162)
is a great spot for a coffee, slice of cake or light
lunch and the courtyard is a real sun-trap.

Sightseeing: You're spoilt for choice with Bahrain
Fort (p.62), the burial mounds (p.64) and Barbar
Temple (p.64).

Shopping: Try Budaiya Highway for independent
shops or the new Country Mall (p.108) for some of
the bigger brands.

Families: A walk around Karbabad, the 'painted
village', near Bahrain Fort (p.62) is great for kids
and snap-happy parents.

Bottom: House and Mosque in Saar Village

Muharraq

It's the first place you see when you land but don't wait until the return flight before visiting these architectural gems.

Muharraq is a large island off the north-eastern tip of Bahrain and it is connected by three main causeways. The international airport occupies the top half of the island, while the industrial southern portion is home to the Khalifa Bin Salman Port and the dry docks. There is the ASRY beach but it's not very clean and the proximity to the powerstation and busy harbour means the water is likely to be polluted.

History buffs and art fans will love Muharraq but otherwise, there isn't a great deal to do here. Visitor attractions include the historical Shaikh Isa Bin Ali House (p.71), and the Pearl Merchant's house (Bait Sayadi p.70). The Mövenpick hotel (p.31) offers some great drinking and fine dining choices as well as a popular pool with grassy areas. With some fine examples of old Arabian architecture, narrow lanes, and traditional shopping areas, Muharraq seems a world away from the modern Bahrain visible just across the water.

For restaurants and bars in the area, see Best Of The Rest p.164

Al Oraifi Museum

1733 5616

Building 374, Road 214, Muharraq

Leading Bahraini artist Rashid Al Oraifi was the first Bahraini to open his own gallery in his home country. He has now opened a museum and art gallery to display works of art

Arabian Gulf

AMWAJ ISLAND

DAIR

SAMAHEEJ

GALALI

Aradous Hwy

11 Ave

Bahrain International Airport

AL BUSAYTIN

Kubra Gardens

4 Al Oraifi Museum

Mövenpick

Airport Ave

MUHARRAQ

2 Bait Sayadi

Shaikh Isa Bin Ali House

1

Arad Hwy

40 Ave

ARAD

Al Neif Hwy

44 Ave

Arad Fort

3

28 Ave

Al Jazayir Ave

Al Fardan Ave

38 Ave

46 Ave

46 Ave

Halim Al Zar Ave

Ibn Qrok Hwy

HIDD

0   1:71,000   2km

and sculptures from the Dilmun era. The gallery also houses a collection of Al Oraifi's own paintings that are inspired by the Dilmun period. More of Al Oraifi's paintings are on display in his gallery, which is in the Bahrain Commercial Complex behind the Sheraton Complex (p.32). Map E 4

Arad Fort
West of Arad Village, Muharraq

Built at the end of the 15th century, the fort is interesting because of the use of traditional local materials in its restoration. Its location on the edge of the bay opposite Bahrain International Airport is quite picturesque, but although it is signposted from Al Hidd Highway, there is no indication of which way to go after that. After leaving the highway, you should take the first right turn at the small roundabout and follow the road round to the left. The entry fee is 200 fils, but quite often the ticket kiosk is empty. During the winter months, handicraft stalls are set up in the courtyard between the fort and the sea, and it has been the setting for many of the Spring Of Culture (p.20) events. Map E 3

Bait Sayadi   1733 4945
Nr Shaikh Isa Bin Ali House, Muharraq

Bait Sayadi (also known as the Pearl Merchant's House) is particularly interesting because of its height, the intricate external and internal decoration and stained glass windows. The house belonged to a pearl merchant in the 19th century and was renovated in 1974. In the future there are plans to use it as a pearl diving museum. Map E 2

Shaikh Isa Bin Ali House

Shaikh Isa Bin Ali House

1733 4945

Shk Abdulla Avenue, Muharraq

This could be one of the highlights of your tour; Shaikh Isa Bin Ali House was built in 1800 and used as a residence until the early 1900s. The house, which has three internal courtyards and 29 rooms on the ground floor, is most notable for its functioning windtower, an early form of air conditioning.

The courtyards are surrounded by archways and the house was built using traditional materials such as sea rock, plaster, lime and palm trunks. The entrance fee is 200 fils and there is a good leaflet in English with plans and photographs. Map E 1

If you only do one thing in...

Muharraq

Step back in time and see some traditional architecture – a million miles away from the modern offerings over the water.

Best for...

Eating & Drinking: The Mövenpick Hotel has fantastic seafood buffets at Silk's restaurant (p.164) on Mondays and renowned Friday brunches. Flamingo bar (p.166) next door has some great live music too.

Sightseeing: See traditional Bahraini architecture at Shaikh Isa Bin Ali House (p.71) and local art by Rashid Al Oraifi (p.68).

Shopping: Don't forget to pick up some duty-free at the airport – you don't need a licence to buy alcohol in Bahrain but it can be expensive.

Families: Exploring Arad Fort (p.70) can be really fun, especially when it's quiet.

Clockwise from top left: Muharraq Souq, Muharraq Mosque, Shaikh Isa Bin Ali House and Muharraq Mosque

73

Central Bahrain

Driving further out of the city you'll see where Bahrainis live and expats play – and maybe a few dolphins too.

The middle of the island can feel pretty remote but there are a few towns and villages to explore on the way to the coast that offer some cultural respite from the desert plains, not to mention the numerous roadside burial mounds. Awali is Bahrain's city of oil and once the place everyone wanted to live but as natural resources declined, so did life in this expat town – but it's still worth a look. Nearby Riffa is where many of the Royal family call home so you can spot some enormous estates, complete with camel farms, all enclosed by seemingless endless fences.

The Al Bander Hotel & Resort (p.76) and nearby islands such as Al Dar (p.76) provide an action-packed getaway with watersports and decent beaches, as well as the chance to spot some dolphins and even the odd turtle. Meanwhile Riffa Golf Club (p.79) is Bahrain's only green golf course.

If shopping is your thing then head to Isa Town for the weekend market (p.78) where you'll can find everything from cassette players to colouring books or support Bahrain's local industries at Al Jasrah (p.76 & p.77), where you can discover some unique souvenirs and get a flavour of village life on the island from the people who live there.

This somewhat barren area is often overlooked by visitors and expats alike but to escape the tourist traps, get the map out and start exploring.

*For **restaurants and bars** in the area, see Best Of The Rest p.164*

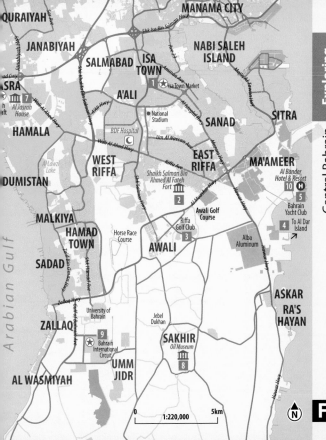

QURAIYAH

JANABIYAH

SALMABAD

MANAMA CITY

ISA TOWN

NABI SALEH ISLAND

Shk Isa Bin Salman Hwy

A'ALI

Amanda Ave

1 ★ Isa Town Market

Awoli Hwy

● National Stadium

SANAD

SITRA

BDF Hospital ☪

Wali Al Ahed Hwy

Um Al Nassan Ave

HAMALA

Al Lawzi Lake

WEST RIFFA

Riffa Ave

EAST RIFFA

MA'AMEER

DUMISTAN

Shaikh Salman Bin Ahmed Al Fateh Fort

2

Al Bander Hotel & Resort

10 Ⓗ

Shk Isa Hwy

Awali Golf Course

Bahrain Yacht Club

5

MALKIYA

Horse Race Course

Riffa Golf Club

3

4 To Al Dar Island

HAMAD TOWN

Alba Aluminum

AWALI

SADAD

Zallaq Hwy

University of Bahrain

Jebel Dukhan

ASKAR

RA'S HAYAN

ZALLAQ

9 ★ Bahrain International Circuit

SAKHIR Oil Museum

8

UMM JIDR

AL WASMIYAH

0   5km

1:220,000

N

F

Arabian Gulf

HSRA

🏛 7

Al Jasrah House

raft

Janabiyah Hwy

ad Cwy

Zallaq Hwy/Shk Khalifa Bin Salman Hwy

Al Bander Hotel & Resort

Nxt Bahrain Yacht Club, Sitra

1770 1201

www.albander.com

For adventurous thrill seekers this hotel resort provides boats and equipment for waterskiing, windsurfing, knee-boarding and sailing. Banana tube ride, rowing boats, canoes, pedalo boats, boat trips and fishing are all available. You will also find a six-lane bowling alley, billiard and snooker tables, table tennis, squash courts and a choice of bars and restaurants. Map F 10

Al Dar Island

3988 3757

Off the East Coast, South of Sitra

This tiny man-made island resort was opened about 10 years ago and is very popular with young Bahrainis. Sea taxis are available from the Sitra Fishermen Port (that's what the sign says) and cost around BD 2.500 for the 10 minute trip. Phone the island and the boat will be sent to take you over. There is a sandy beach and a restaurant where alcohol is available. Parasailing, waterskiing, fishing trips, banana-boat rides and pedalo boats are all available. Sea swimmers are warned to be extra careful, as there is often a very strong current. Map F 4

Al Jasrah Handicraft Centre

1761 1900

Al Jasrah Village

At Al Jasrah Handicraft Centre you can see different skills such as cloth weaving, palm weaving, pottery and furniture making being practised in separate rooms. The centre runs handicraft courses to train Bahrainis in the traditional crafts and there is a shop that sells examples of their work. Entrance is free. Map F 6

Al Jasrah House

1761 1454

Al Jasrah Village

Al Jasrah House, the late Shaikh Isa's birthplace, was built from local materials in 1907 and is a fine example of traditional architecture. It consists of several small rooms which still have the original furnishings. One of the rooms was used to drain juice from dates which were stacked in palm baskets to become ripe. Entrance is 200 fils. Map F 7

Bahrain International Circuit

1745 0000

Gulf of Bahrain Avenue, Sakhir   www.bahraingp.com

In addition to holding the first Grand Prix in the Middle East, the last few years have seen the BIC grow in many directions. The circuit has hosted a variety of races, corporate activities and functions. In addition, the Formula BMW Performance Centre has been set up and recently held its first Formula BMW Race Professional course with a view to educating Bahraini drivers and giving them a real chance to become international Formula 1 drivers. Non-professionals – or those who fancy their chances on the track – can also have a go as either drivers or passengers. There are open track days if you want to try out your own vehicle but you might want to check the insurance policy on the hire car before signing up! Otherwise, there are some exciting cars waiting to be abused, including Hummers, quadbikes, a Caterham G7 and a Chevrolet to take for a spin on SkidXtreme days. Even if you don't want to get behind the wheel, the tours are popular. Map F 9

Bahrain Yacht Club & Marina   1770 0677
Nxt Al Bander Resort, Sitra   www.bahrainyachtclub.com.bh

If you go on a dolphin-watching trip with the Bahrain Yacht Club
you are entitled to use the club facilities for the rest of the day.
The club offers a privateman-made beach, a swimming pool,
restaurants (p.166), bars and a cafe. There is also a fully-equipped
diving and sailing school. The dolphin trip costs BD 6 for adults
and BD 3 for children under 13 years old; there are three per day
and you'd be advised to book by phone. Map F 5

Isa Town Market
Off Quds Avenue, Isa Town

The Isa Town Market or Souk is known by several names. It is
sometimes called the Souk Al Haraj or the flea market, and
sometimes referred to as the Iranian Market. It is an interesting
local market, used by residents as opposed to tourists, and there
are some good bargains to be had as well as animals for sale
so be warned that the conditions aren't great. There is also a
large discount emporium, Ramez Trading, as part of the market
which is a good place to pick up a cheap suitcase if you've gone
a little overboard on the spending. It is well signposted in the Isa
Town area with signs indicating Isa Town Local Market off Quds
Avenue. Women would do well to cover up. Map F 1

The Oil Museum   1775 3475
Nr Jebel Al Dukhan, Sakhir

This interesting little museum is a long way out of town,
in the midst of the Bahrain oil fields at the foot of Jebel
Dukhan. The turn-off for the museum is signposted

from Zallaq Highway. Theoretically the museum is open from 10:00 to 17:00 on Thursdays and Fridays, but it is advisable to phone before you set out to confirm. Inside there is a fascinating collection of objects related to oil exploration and a wonderful photographic history of the early development of the oil industry in Bahrain. Map F 8

Riffa Golf Club
East of Awali, Riffa

1775 0777
www.riffagolfclub.com

The club has special visitors' golf rates ranging from BD 16 for Night Golf (nine holes) to BD 38 for Weekend Golf (18 holes). Golf clubs, carts, shoes and clothes can be hired fairly cheaply. There are also two restaurants which are open to non-members for lunch and dinner. Map F 3

Shaikh Salman Bin Ahmed Fateh Fort
Nr Hununaiyah Valley, South of Riffa

From its spectacular vantage point, this 19th century fort (also known as Riffa Fort) looks down on a modern housing development of whitewashed houses and it's a great spot for a photo. The fort contains many small rooms, the walls of some of them showing the handprints of the workmen who smoothed the plaster finish. A general leaflet in English and Arabic is available, but the information is somewhat sparse. The fort is open from Saturday to Tuesday from 08:00 to 14:00, Wednesday and Thursday from 09:00 to 18:00 and on Friday from 15:00 to 18:00. Admittance is 200 fils. Access to the fort is from Riffa Avenue and the route is well signposted. Map F 2

If you only do one thing in...

Central Bahrain

Check out the cool design and hot wheels at the Bahrain International Circuit (p.77).

Best for...

Eating & Drinking: Try super fresh fish at the Seafood Hut at Bahrain Yacht Club (p.166).

Sightseeing: Al Jasrah House (p.77) offers a unique insight into the traditional building methods and a simpler way of life – and all for 200 fils!

Shopping: Isa Town Market (p.78) sells everything you could ever want – and quite a few things you wouldn't.

Relaxing: Get away from it all with a trip to Al Dar and the neighbouring islands (p.76).

Families: Try out new watersports at Al Bander Hotel & Resort (p.30) or just enjoy a barbecue and some shisha at their waterfront restaurant.

Clockwise from top: Al Jasrah House, Isa Town Mosque, Handicraft Centre

Southern Bahrain

Everywhere in Bahrain is within an hour's drive but you really feel away from the city once you head south.

The bleak landscape and sparse population belie the amount there is to do away from Manama and you can easily spend a day here. Spa fans will love the new Banyan Tree Desert Spa & Resort, sun-worshippers will appreciate the beach at Bahrain Sailing Club (p.84), below, and kids will be entertained at Al Areen Wildlife Park (p.82). To truly get away from it all, head to Hawar Island for watersports and deserted shores.

Al Areen Wildlife Park   1775 3475
Nr Bahrain International Circuit

Al Areen Wildlife Park is the only nature reserve in Bahrain. Follow the signposts for the International Circuit, then follow the signs to Al Areen. The park covers more than eight square kilometres and has an impressive collection of birds and mammals, albeit in pretty tired conditions. Tickets cost BD 1 for adults and 500 fils for children. The tour takes 45 minutes and starts every hour, on the hour, in an air-conditioned bus with a driver and tour guide, who gives a running commentary in Arabic and English during the tour. Map G 3

Al Jazayer Beach
Approx 8km from Awali, West Coast

Situated on the west coast of Bahrain, several kilometres south-west of Al Areen Wildlife Park, the well-signposted

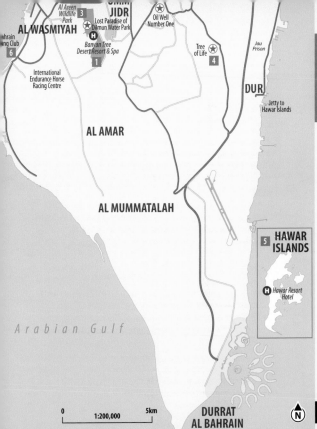

AL WASMIYAH

UMM JIDR

Al Areen Wildlife Park **3**

Lost Paradise of Dilmun Water Park

Oil Well Number One

Tree of Life **4**

H Banyan Tree Desert Resort & Spa **1**

Bahrain Racing Club **6**

International Endurance Horse Racing Centre

AL AMAR

Jau Prison

DUR

Jetty to Hawar Islands

AL MUMMATALAH

5 HAWAR ISLANDS

H Hawar Resort Hotel

Arabian Gulf

DURRAT AL BAHRAIN (U/C)

0   1:200,000   5km

Al Jazayer Beach is one of the few swimming beaches open to the general public. Unfortunately, it's not very clean, the water is very shallow and it has rubbish floating in it. The beach has several small dilapidated beach chalets with bamboo-slatted walls, wooden roofs and power points. The huts can be rented at BD 3 for 24 hours but you probably wouldn't want to be there that long... Map G 2

Bahrain Sailing Club
1783 6078
Al Jazayer Beach, West Coast

Situated next door to the open beach, this sailing club has hosted international regattas and boasts its own, much cleaner, shoreline. It's a neat little complex equipped with swimming pool, watersports, restaurant and a two-storey accommodation building where you can book in for the night or a week. Day visitors are charged a nominal BD 1 fee to use the facilities. Map G 6

Banyan Tree Desert Spa & Resort
1784 5000
Nr Al Areen Wildlife Park
www.banyantree.com/bahrain

This resort is a haven of luxury and peace. It is the only all-villa complex in Bahrain, offering world-class restaurants and 78 private residences, each with its own pool. The 10,000 square metre spa is the largest of its kind in the Middle East, with an extensive range of luxurious therapies to guests and visitors alike. Non-guests can dine at the restaurants which provide a unique night away from Manana. Situated only five minutes from Bahrain International Circuit, this retreat offers the finest possible treatments in sumptuous surroundings. Map G 1

Hawar Island
Approx 20km south-east of Bahrain

If you've dreamt of stepping ashore a fantasy desert island, Hawar could be just the place. It is in fact much closer to Qatar than Bahrain and 'ownership' of the island was debated for years. Possibly the biggest attraction is the Hawar Resort Hotel (1748 9111, www.hawarresort.com), with lots of recreational, dining and entertaiment facilities. The resort runs a speedboat shuttle service between the island and Dur on the mainland which 45 minute. Map G 5

Tree of Life
South-East of Jebel Dukhan

One of Bahrain's best-known natural wonders is the Tree of Life, alone in the otherwise barren desert south-east of Jebel Dukhan. Its source of water a mystery. The tree is estimated to be 400 years old, much older than the normal acacia 150 year lifespan. It is signposted from Al Muaskar Highway, but after Riffa Golf Club signs are rare between so follow the small green signs for the Shaikh Isa Air Base. The tree has suffered at the hands of its fans and is covered in graffiti so don't be disappointed. Map G 4

Paradise Found

One of the latest additions to Southern Bahrain is the Lost Paradise of Dilmun. It opened in late 2007 and is the largest water park in the Middle East, featuring a wave pool and many slides. It is closed during the winter months but for more information visit www.lpodwaterpark.com.

If you only do one thing in...

Southern Bahrain

Go to the Tree of Life to see what all the fuss is about.

Best for...

Sightseeing: The drive alone offers a great insight into life in this part of Bahrain – keep an eye out for the 'nodding donkey' oil pumps near Oil Well Number One.

Relaxation: Unwind on the beach on Hawar Island (p.85) or head to the treatment rooms at the Banyan Tree Desert Spa & Resort (p.84).

Families: Learn about Bahrain's flora and fauna and take a trip to Al Areen Wildlife Park (p.82).

Outdoor: Bahrain Sailing Club (p.84) has the best natural beach on the main island.

Clockwise from top left: Al Areen Wildlife Park, Dhow on the West Coast, Tree of Life

Tours & Sightseeing

An organised tour can be one of the best ways to experience Bahrain. Your hotel may be able to arrange a special deal or choose from these options to find the trip that best suits your needs.

City Tours

Although Manama city centre is relatively small, some insider knowledge (and navigation skills) can make a big difference. The companies below offer trips around the city, plus some sights a little further out, so they're ideal if you're only in Bahrain for a short stay.

Dadabhai Travel   1722 6650

Dadabhai Travel's Shopping Tour visits Manama Souk, Seef Mall and Al Aali Shopping Complex. The tour takes three hours and ranges from BD 11 per person (for two to five people), down to BD 7 per person for 25 or more people. They also have what they call a City Tour, which not only goes to Bahrain Fort but also to King Fahad Causeway and the Camel Farm. The tour takes two and a half hours and ranges from BD 12 per person (for two to five people), down to BD 7 per person for 25 or more people.

Oasis Travel   1781 3713

Oasis Travel offers a half-day Culture & Tradition Tour every day except Friday and Saturday, which takes in Al Khamis Mosque, Beit Al Qur'an, Muharraq Souk, Shaikh Isa Bin Ali House,

Bait Sayadi and Arad Fort. Their half-day Fascinating Capital Tour (every day except Monday and Friday) visits the fish and vegetable markets, the Al Fateh Mosque, the National Museum, Bab Al Bahrain and the Manama Souk. Tours cost BD 20 per person for adults (for a minimum of four people), and BD 10 per child.

Boat Tours

Several companies offer boat tours such as dolphin-watching trips, lunch and dinner cruises, and swimming and snorkelling trips, in addition to the regular speedboat journey to the Hawar Islands. The islands, which were once described by an over-enthusiastic government official as 'The Maldives of the Gulf' are, in fact, flat barren treeless deserts. There is nowhere to go outside the hotel grounds, so one tends to laze in the pool soaking up the peaceful atmosphere (and any beverage that comes to hand) or get active with the watersports.

Island Tours' air-conditioned, luxury, 51 foot yacht takes you out to Jaradah Island, where you can swim or ride on a jetski, which is carried on board. The evening cruise leaves at 18:00 and lasts for two hours. See page 51 for more details.

Dadabhai Travel (1722 6650) can arrange dhow trips for BD 10 for adults and BD 5 for children, based on a minimum of 15 passengers. Trips, which are available on request, include a continental lunch or dinner.

Boats to the Hawar Islands leave the Dur Jetty at 10:00 each morning. The return trip costs BD 12 per passenger. After a bumpy 45 minute ride you are met at the Hawar Resort jetty and taken on a five-minute journey round the lagoon to the hotel, where you are greeted. A buffet lunch is served at 12:30 (get there early, as there is a limited choice of food and it runs out fairly quickly if there's a big crowd). Jetskis, pedalo boats and canoes can be hired and boats return to the mainland at 17:30. For bookings and more information, phone 1729 0377.

Gulf Discovery (p.50) is also able to provide dhow cruises tailored to your requirements or for a dinner cruise see page 140 for excursions with Jean-Pierre Cohen.

Dolphin & Whale Watching
The Bahrain Yacht Club (p.78) runs three dolphin-watching trips every day. Weather permitting, boats leave the club at 10:00, 12:00 and 14:00. The trip costs BD 6 for adults and BD 3 for children under 13, and lasts about an hour and a half. It's a good idea to phone again the day before you go to check if anybody else has booked, as there is a minimum charge of BD 24 per boat. The fee entitles you to spend the rest of the day enjoying the club facilities and restaurants.

Island Tours (p.51) offers three types of boat trip which leave from the Marina Club on Al Fatih Highway: dolphin watching, a lunchtime island trip and an evening cruise. The dolphin-watching trips leave at 10:00, 12:00 and 14:00 every day and last for two hours. The charge is BD 8 for adults and BD 4 for children, and soft drinks are provided. Phone 1729 4439 for bookings and more information.

Mosque Tours
Al Fateh Mosque, commonly known as the Grand Mosque, is on the seaward side of Al Fatih Highway. This enormous building with its huge dome can accommodate 7,000

Al Fateh Mosque

worshippers in the main prayer hall, balconies and courtyard. Non-Muslims can visit at any time, except during prayer time, from Sunday to Thursday between 09:00 and 17:00, provided they are suitably dressed. Nobody wearing shorts is admitted and ladies can borrow an abaya to wear when entering the prayer hall. Knowledgeable guides are available to conduct you around the mosque, which is a beautiful example of Islamic architecture. During Eid there are special tours for non-Muslims with educational talks, henna painting and Arabic calligraphy.

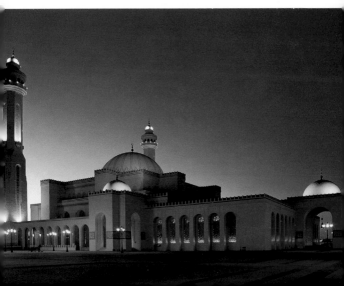

Sports & Spas

Sports & Activities

Whatever your bag, be it extreme sports or total relaxation, there's plenty to keep you busy on this action-packed island.

Bahrain has a small but diverse population with a number of different cultures making up the scene. This means that you don't need to look too far to find something to keep you busy during your stay with sports and activities or just some good old fashioned relaxing.

Visitors may be surprised by the sudden transition from summer to winter and back again. It usually happens overnight and temperatures can leap or plummet between 10 and 15°C. In the summer months, activity is restricted to indoor, air-conditioned facilities such as the EZ FIT Sportsplex (Budaiya, 1769 2378) where cricket lovers can play indoor or to outdoor, floodlit venues such as the Riffa Golf Club (see p.79) where golf-crazy aficionados swarm to the course at sundown. In winter, temperatures are comfortably within the 18 to 25° range so that outdoor sports and activities can be enjoyed at any time of the day.

Being an island nation, sailing is a popular weekend pastime. There are many small islands close by where you can get away from it all and discover remote beaches where the shallow waters are packed with marine life; perfect for diving, snorkelling and fishing. Sailing clubs also act as social clubs and are a great way to meet people and enjoy a variety of activities and events. See the table on page 99 for details.

Indoor sports such as bowling and ice skating are popular when the sun is beating down; Funland (p.50) offers both activities and provides welcome respite from the summer heat.

If you have visited the Formula One International Circuit (see p.77) and are feeling inspired to get behind a set of (somewhat smaller) wheels then pay a visit to a karting centre. There are several on the island including Gulf Speed One (3944 4137) near Citibank in Seef and Rally Town in Janabiyah (1761 2992), which also has a mini golf course. Sessions cost from BD 2 depending on your choice of motor, although the chances are you won't find a Ferrari around here.

For some truly outdoor activity, pack up the hire car and go camping. Whether on the beaches or in the desert, camping is the best way of getting clear views of the starry Arabian night skies. There are no official campgrounds in Bahrain, so it's just a case of pitching up well away from habitation and making sure you're not on private land.

Life's Not A Beach

Despite Bahrain being made up of a group of small islands, there are very few pleasant beaches. This is due to factors like the shallow seas, stony shorelines and the illegal dumping of rubbish. The best beaches are man-made and belong to clubs and hotels such as The Ritz-Carlton (p.59) and Bahrain Sailing Club (p.84) but plans are afoot to create some good public beaches in the future.

Watersports & Diving

If it has anything to do with water, above or below, you can bet that the warm seas of the islands offer it all.

There's a lot of sporty, watery fun to be had in Bahrain; choose from slow and soothing, like sailing on the open water, to something to get your blood racing like kitesurfing or jetskiing.

With Bahrain being an island, it's hardly surprising that sailing is one of the most popular pursuits. The kingdom is surrounded by numerous small islands, some of which are only visible at low tide. These get washed clean every day and many boat owners head here for the pristine conditions as the tide goes out. Dolphins are regular visitors to Bahrain and a number of organisations provide Dolphin Watch Boats.

The history of diving in Bahrain is among the most ancient and lucrative in the world, with over 4,200 years in the pearl diving trade. As a result, there is a wide range of wrecks dotted about the reefs and the coasts of Bahrain. The temperature of the sea encourages diving almost all year round, ranging from a comfortable 20 to 34°C in summer. Wetsuits are worn from November to April, while Lycra suits are usually sufficient during the summer - although you have to be pretty brave to bear the conditions once it hits 40°C and upwards. Visibility is very good for offshore dives, averaging around 25 metres and reducing to five metres inshore.

There are over 200 species of fish and around 30 species of coral to look out for including rays, moray eels, crayfish, trigger fish, clown fish, turtles and sturgeon on the reef and mackerel, cobia, tuna and barracuda. Popular dive spots include the pearl diving sites where you may even get lucky and find your own.

Fishing is undoubtedly big here, as you'll see from the number of fishermen hanging out lines from the Sitra causeway. The shallow waters around the island teem with Spanish mackerel but hammour is just as easily found out in the deeper holes in the reef areas. Most of the inner reefs have been fished out now so most fishermen go out some 5-10 kilometres to trawl with rapellas or fish with live bait and sinkers for sharri, barracuda, kingfish and needlefish.

The shallow waters also make kayaking the perfect way to visit some of the other islands within the archipelago. You can hire them from most of the beach hotels or beach resorts for around BD 4 per hour for two people.

Jetskiing is also enjoyed by a large number of people here and most of the beach hotels such as the Ritz-Carlton Bahrain Hotel & Spa, the Novotel Al Dana Resort, the Al Bander Hotel & Resort and Hawar Resort Hotel have equipment for hire. See table opposite.

If you're looking for a real buzz, kitesurfing is arguably the number one activity on the water these days. The Amwaj Islands, behind the International Airport, is currently one of the favourite locations and it looks as though the new development on the island may give the go ahead for the sport to take place there. For more information on kitesurfing in Bahrain, contact the Skate Shack (1769 7176) or visit their website at www.skate-shack.com.

Al Bander Hotel & Resort
www.albander.com

Nr Bahrain Yacht Club, Sitra Phone: 1770 1201
Parasailing, jetskiing, water skiing, sailing, windsurfing

Aqua Hobbies
www.aqua-hobbies.com

Palace Ave, Ras Romman Phone: 1729 3231
Diving

Aquatique

Government Ave, Na'im Phone: 1727 1780
Diving, snorkelling

Bahrain Sailing Club

Al Jazayer Beach, West Coast Phone: 1783 6078
Sailing

Bahrain Yacht Club & Marina
www.bahrainyachtclub.com.bh

Nr Al Bander Resort, Sitra Phone: 1770 0677
Diving, fishing, boat hire, jetskiing, dolphin watching tours

Hawar Resort Hotel
www.hawarresort.com

Hawar Island Phone: 1784 9111
Jetskiing, snorkelling, pedalos, kayaking

Island Tours

Marina Club, Hoora Phone: 1771 0088
Dolphin watching tours, island trips, boat cruises

Marina Club
www.marinaclub.info

Off Al Fatih Highway, Hoora Phone: 1729 1527
Parasailing, boat trips, jetskiing

Novotel Al Dana Resort
www.novotel-bahrain.com

Off Shk Hamad Causeway Phone: 1729 8008
Jetskiing, waterskiing, windsurfing, kayaking

The Ritz-Carlton Hotel & Spa
www.ritzcarlton.com

Off King Abdulla The Second Ave, Seef Phone: 1758 0000
Parasailing, jetskiing, waterskiing, boat trips, fishing

Zallaq Sailing Club

End of Zallaq Highway, West Coast Phone: 1783 6078
Boat charter

Spas & Well-Being

Once the chaos of the islands is quelled, get pampered, massaged and soothed back to your normal self.

If it's time to look after number one, Bahrain is the place to be. There are an abundance of spas, salons, gyms, clubs and fitness centres. You can indulge yourself at an expensive five-star spa or enjoy treatments in one of the very reasonably priced smaller salons. Services on offer include all the usual beauty treatments; manicures, pedicures, facials, every type of massage, nail services, hair removal and detoxifying treatments to name but a few.

Beauty is big business in Bahrain. All of the major hotels have beauty salons, usually popular with the expats but more expensive than the smaller salons. If you go to an Arabic women's salon make sure not to bring your husband anywhere near it as they have a very strict no-men-allowed-at-all policy. The traditional practice of painting henna on the hands and feet is still very popular with Bahraini women and a design can make for a great memento – it's quite cheap and the intricate brown patterns fade after a few weeks.

For sheer indulgence, or just for health and therapeutic reasons, you can't beat a good massage. You can experience everything from a totally decadent pampering massage to reflexology, aromatherapy and Chinese massage, all at very reasonable prices.

Banyan Tree Desert Spa & Resort   1784 5000
Nr Al Areen Wildlife Park   www.banyantree.com/bahrain

This is the first venture in Bahrain for the Singapore-based chain of luxury spas and one to watch out for. It is the most extensive spa in the Middle East, offering a huge range of body and beauty treatments in luxurious surroundings including 12 spa treatment rooms, self scrub cabin, grotto steam cabin, ice igloo, garden hammam, herbal steam room, brine cavern and an assortment of 'experience' showers! Map 1-C5

Bodyline   1779 3932
Off Budaiya Highway, Saar

Beauty and body treatments are offered in a beautifully designed spa that features a Moroccan Bath, fully-equipped gym, indoor swimming pool and squash court. There is also the option of Pilates, aromatherapy massage and Thai massage plus they provide health foods to go. Map 1-B2

Jacques Dessange   1771 3999
Nr Al Bustan Hotel, Adliya   www.jacques-dessange.com

Jacques Dessange offers total pampering and has something to suit everybody in its luxurious ladies spa, hair salon and health club. There is a spacious, fully-equipped gym with exercise machines designed with women in mind, and there is also a range of m massages available including aromatic oil (with inclusive foot massage), full body and Thai massage. Map 2-G4

La Fontaine Centre of Contemporary Art

92 Hoora Avenue, Hoora

1723 0123

www.lafontaineartcentre.com

This spa, set in a historic house in Hoora, oozes an atmosphere of peace and tranquillity. There is a restaurant, art gallery and a pool as well as the spa's offerings of full beauty treatments and specialist massages. Particularly impressive is the state-of-the-art women-only spa with its exclusive Jean Marc Sinan skin care line, body treatments, slimming technology (Ultrasonolipolysis), along with Pilates, aromatherapy, weight loss and detoxifying treatments. Map 2-G2

Pineapple Spa

Nr Al Bustan Hotel, Adliya

1771 2000

The Pineapple Spa offers a great range of massages, facials and beauty treatments including hair removal; the threading is particularly good. It also has a hair salon and a gym with good parking facilities just off the main road. Map 2-G4

Royal Spa

Ritz-Carlton, Bahrain Hotel & Spa, Seef

1758 6808

www.ritzcarlton.com

The Royal Spa is located in the five-star Ritz-Carlton, Bahrain Hotel and Spa. Their various holistic, traditional or contemporary techniques care for the whole being of a person and all treatments are available for men and women, including a particularly impressive range of massages. ESPA & Guinot treatments and products are also available. Map 2-C1

Shopping

Shopping In Bahrain

A choice of malls, souks and independent shops make Bahrain the perfect place to spend those dinars.

As shopping paradises go, Bahrain is not exactly a world-renowned destination, but there's plenty here to delight even the most dedicated spendaholic. Shopping is one of the major leisure activities in Bahrain and whatever your purchase preferences, you'll find them well catered for. From window shopping in the upmarket, designer-label boutiques to rummaging through fabulous bargains in huge discount emporiums or trawling for treasures in the souk, Bahrain has it all.

Prices vary a lot depending on the quality or quantity of what you're buying, and in the souks and small retail stores your bargaining skills will also affect the price. On an international level, there aren't really any bargains in Bahrain. Computers and electronic goods are generally cheaper in Dubai or in south-east Asia and designer label clothes are as expensive, or more expensive, than in the UK or the US. The real joy of shopping in Bahrain is the variety offered and the chance of stumbling upon a really special item or genuine bargain. Recommended buys are gold, pearls, carpets and antique Arabic furniture.

The major malls are located in the Seef district; Al Aali Shopping Complex (p.108) and Seef Mall (p.110) are within walking distance of each other, but with a major road bisecting the area, travelling by car (or taxi) is essential if you want to visit the other big malls. The souks are well worth a visit; not just for the shopping, but also for the atmosphere. Generally retailers are not too pushy and your shopping experience is guaranteed to be an interesting one.

If you are bartering for a bargain, remember department stores, supermarkets and international shops have fixed prices and trying to haggle there will be seen as bad form. However, you can flex your bargaining muscles in the souks or independent shops (especially those selling electronics, antiques and jewellery). Simply asking 'is that your best price?' with a smile can get good results, and if all else fails the usual shake of the head and walking out the door can have the desired effect. Remember that settling on a price is akin to a verbal agreement to buy the item, so do your research on prices first and shop around to ensure you are truly getting a bargain.

Refunds & Exchanges

The key to getting refunds and making exchanges is the same as everywhere else in the world. Make sure that you keep your original receipts, especially for big-ticket items. The large international stores all have reasonable and clearly defined policies. For purchases made in other stores, the policy will depend on the shop owner; if it is an expensive item, find out what the rules are before you buy to avoid any problems in the future.

Al Aali Shopping Complex

1758 1000

Nxt Seef Mall, Seef

Al Aali is retail heaven if you need to satisfy your lust for designer labels. Located alongside Seef Mall, and with its distinctive Arabic architecture, it has established itself as a true shoppers' destination and one of the country's tourist attractions. Al Aali embodies the spirit of today along with the heritage of the past, featuring superior designers such as Gucci and Jimmy Choo alongside outlets selling traditional Arabic wares. Also worth visiting is THE One, for their luxury living ideas and a fantastic cafe (see p.156). Map 2-C2

Bahrain Mall

1755 8100

Opp Seef Mall, Sanabis

Bahrain Mall has a distinctive, pink-brick, fortress style of architecture. It is currently the only mall to have a hypermarket; the large and hugely popular Geant, where an amazing range of goods is available. The mall has 120 retailers and targets middle-of-the-road family shoppers. There is a great play area for kids called Foton World (see p.59) and a large foodcourt selling all the western and Arabic favourites. Nearly all of the parking is undercover and it has a post office on the ground floor. Map 2-C3

Country Mall

Budaiya Highway, Saar

This brand new mall is set to be a favourite among expats living in the area, but the range of cafes and shops (including Birkenstock's flagship store on the island) also

THE BAHRAIN MALL
مجمع البحرين

make it a great spot to stop off on the way to some of the nearby forts and sights. Map 1-C2

Dana Mall   1755 8500
Nr Shk Khalifa Bin Salman Highway, Sanabis

The anchor store in Dana Mall is called Giant, which is not related in any way to Geant, the hypermarket in Bahrain Mall, just up the road. Confused? It is confusing for visitors and newcomers to Bahrain. However, Giant in Dana Mall is a much smaller store. The shops are nothing to write home about so the main attractions are the luxurious cinema complex, the mini amusement park for children Chakazoolu (see p.58), the excellent restaurants and the Arabian-style foodcourt. Map 2-D3

Marina Mall   1727 7800
Nxt Fish Market, City Centre

Marina Mall is a family shopping complex with a group of medium-sized stores selling good value items for the family. The major stores are Home Centre, Mothercare, Shoe Mart, Sarah's Secret, Nine West and Splash. There are a couple of good coffee shops and foodcourts. The kids will love the Jungle foodcourt and you will love its bargain prices. Map 2-E3

Seef Mall   1758 1111
Opp Bahrain Mall, Seef

Seef Mall is currently the biggest and probably the most popular mall in Bahrain, complete with over 250 shops, four large department stores, two foodcourts, a children's entertainment centre and two cinema complexes. It is modern, air conditioned, has a huge parking area and all the other services you would expect in a large international shopping mall. Fashion is probably the main focus of the mall, especially with the new extension which includes Forever 21, Banana Republic, Hobbs, Tommy Hilfiger, Dune, Gap and Sephora for cosmetics. Other shops include Debehams, Oasis, Topshop, Jashanmal Bookstore and Marks & Spencer. Map 2-C2

Sitra Mall

Off Majlis Tawon Highway, Sitra

There appears to be a disproportionate number of shops full of baby and children's clothes here, but this new mall shouldn't be discounted. It has a large foodcourt with all the usual suspects present, a supermarket, an indoor recreation area, a large covered carpark and over 100 shops (although not all are occupied yet). It's usually pretty quiet too, so you can enjoy the light and airy atmosphere in peace.

In The Future...

Bahrain City Centre, a giant shopping and leisure complex with indoor water park, is due to open in 2008 and you can see the progress on the World Trade Center and Financial Harbour with every passing day. Manama's skyline is looking more and more like neighbouring Dubai's so it's an exciting time to watch it all happen.

Hotspots

Venturing out of the air-conditioned comfort of the malls might be a scary prospect, but the shopping rewards can be well worth it.

Apart from the shopping malls in Manama, there are plenty of interesting shopping spots all over Bahrain. Exhibition Avenue, in Hoora, and Adliya are two popular areas in the centre of the city, see below for more details. For a more cultural experience, you can also check out the souks and markets such as Manama Souk, Central Market or the Gold Souk (see p.115).

If you're in the homeware market, then take a trip down Budaiya Highway for lots of independent stores selling pottery as well as the new Country Mall, which has a Birkenstock store and lots of dining options. As well as these, all of the towns and villages outside Manama have their own unique shopping area, so you can soak up the local atmosphere while bagging a bargain.

Exhibition Avenue

Hoora

Ok, so the traffic can be a nightmare, and you might not want to take a stroll here after dark, but if you're looking for cheap electronics then Exhibition Avenue is the place to be. The neon lights, cruising cars and vibrant atmosphere make it a welcome change from the often sterile malls and you're bound to pick up a bargain or ten. Head to the GOSI Complex (which has a car park at the back) for mobile phones or the Apple outlet over the road, which does repairs if your iPod has had an untimely melt-down. There are also loads of fastfood restaurants around the clock tower roundabout for that much-needed mid-shop energy boost. Map 2-G2

Adliya

A favourite with locals and visitors alike, Adliya has a bit of a holiday vibe and it's a great place to wander around before dinner at one of the many fantastic restaurants in the area. The focus is on carpets, antiques and jewellery, so get your bargaining skills at the ready for the many independent shops lining the main street. One place also worth a visit is GAB (Gulf Antiques Bahrain) in the Caesar building near the Ferrari garage, which is great for gorgeous home accessories like glass lanterns, cushion covers and crockery. Map 2-G4

Souks & Markets

Get your wallet at the ready, Bahrain's souks are a shopper's paradise offering everything from spices to sequins.

The word 'souk' is Arabic for 'market', and there are many interesting souks, both modern and traditional, in Bahrain. The best known is Manama Souk (opposite), which has several areas selling textiles, spices, jewellery, perfumes, electronics and a wide assortment of goods, both practical and ornamental, within a maze of narrow lanes and alleyways. It also houses the large and popular Gold City (opposite) with its vast range of glittering 18 or 21 carat gold jewellery.

The Central Market is the place to go for fresh fruit, vegetables, meat and fish, while Isa Town Market (p.78) is known as the flea market of Bahrain and is a great place for bargain hunters. Bargaining is expected in all of the souks so don't be afraid to have a haggle. As with all Middle Eastern countries, women should cover up to avoid unwanted attention.

Souvenirs

Apart from gold, pearls, art, antiques and authentic Arabic homewares such as wooden chests, model dhows, pottery, woven baskets and carpets make memorable and unique souvenirs. There's also a plethora of mosque clocks and camel-related gifts for something a little sillier for the folks at home. See p.118 for some of Bahrain's best buys, or try the excellent selection in the Duty Free shop at the airport.

Central Market
Nr Pearl Roundabout, City Centre
Get up early and wear sensible shoes. That's all you
really need to know about this food market near the
Pearl roundabout! You'll see merchants shifting fresh
fish, fruit and vegetables from dawn and even if you're
not shopping, it's a great experience. Just don't go
too late in the day as it can get a bit smelly... It's well
signposted from the highway but if you get lost look for
Marina Mall; they share a carpark. Map 2-E3

Gold City
Manama Souk, City Centre
Gold City is amazing! Shop after shop, row after row of
gold: necklaces, earrings, rings, bracelets, huge, ornately-
crafted Arabic neck and head pieces.... It is bewildering
to decide what to buy. The majority of the items are
18 or 21 carat gold and they carry a hallmark. You can
also get a piece of jewellery custom-made to your own
design. Take a picture or photo with you and chat to
the goldsmiths. It's advisable to know the current gold
prices and negotiate a price before you place an order
or buy anything. Map 3-A2

Manama Souk
Nr Bab Al Bahrain, City Centre
You enter Manama Souk through the old seaport gate,
Bab Al Bahrain. The seafront has been reclaimed and
is now quite some distance away, but the bustling

traditional souk remains. Don't even think of taking a car; the roads are narrow and very busy, and it is easy to get lost or trapped in a dead-end street with no way to turn or back out. The souk is divided into areas, the most well known of which is Gold City (see p.115).

There is also a textile souk, the traditional gold souk with lots of antiques, an aromatic spice souk and a tin souk, but everything is sold here, including cheap clothing, electrical goods and some interesting souvenirs. You will find stalls selling traditional herbs, leaf tobacco, local craft items and all sorts of fascinating odds and ends. You will be expected to barter and most stallholders will not accept credit cards, so take plenty of dinars (in a range of denominations) but don't flash your cash around. Women might be advised to stay away at night; while it is safe, there's plenty of staring and some harmless but uncomfortable following around too.

Map 3-B2

Shisha Pipes

A great gift for your laidback friends, the iconic shisha pipe can be bought cheaply from the souk and larger supermarkets like Geant at Bahrain Mall (see p.108). For a greater choice head to Adliya where you'll see the highly-decorated pipes sold alongside carpets, pottery and antique jewellery. The fruity tobacco, which comes in a variety of flavour, is also widely available – just be aware that it's not that good for your health.

Clockwise from top left: Manama Gold Souq, Tobacco Seller, Textile Souq, Fish Market

Art

Bahrain has a thriving art scene, with some of the most well-established galleries and shops in the Gulf. Arabesque Art Gallery (p.48), has been established for nearly 30 years and showcases local art and the scenes of artist Wahab Al Koheji. Another well-known gallery is Dar Albareh Art Gallery in Umm al Hassam (1771 3535). There are also numerous framing shops, which also sell a wide variety of mass-produced prints and paintings.

Carpets

Carpets are a best-selling item in Bahrain and pieces originating from Iran, India, Pakistan, China and Asia are all available. The main shopping street in Adliya is lined with carpet shops, all with similar stock, but as each carpet is unique, take your time when selecting one to buy. If you are considering spending serious money, do some research about where the carpet was made, who made it and test the quality. Certificates of authenticity are available for higher priced carpets, and Isam at Tehran Handmade Carpets in Adliya is always good for genuine advice. Isa Town Market (p.78) also has a large number of carpet shops, which sell a wide selection of lower-priced, machine-made rugs.

Gold & Jewellery

You're spoilt for choice for gold in Bahrain; all the big designer names are here, but the real bargains are at the Gold City (see p.115), where you can choose from the dazzling displays or get a piece custom made. Gold is sold by weight, so it pays to check out the current rate in newspapers before you go shopping. You also need to consider the workmanship when pricing an item. Pearls are also a great purchase in Bahrain and you should buy the best you can afford – but buying what you like is more important than making a financial investment.

Perfumes

It's a fun experience to shop for perfume in the speciality Arabic shops in the malls, and it can make a great gift or souvenir. First choose a bottle from a large selection of delightful, ornate designs. Then you'll need to choose your fragrance, and once again the range is vast. The sales people are very knowledgeable about their products, and it can be as cheap or as expensive as you wish to make it. These shops also usually sell incense and incense burners.

Textiles

There is an excellent choice from quality velvets to cotton and silk, and from inexpensive imported Liberty Prints (Mohamed Jamal in Al Aali Shopping Complex) to cheap cotton prints and suit fabric from India. The best place to start is probably the textile section of the Manama Souk (Map 3-B2). There are also good selections in fabric shops in the Old Palace Road area, Lulu Centre and in the main out of town shopping areas like Riffa, Isa Town and Hamad Town. The main shopping malls have some fabric shops, where the prices are higher, but in the heat of summer it may be better to pay a little more for the luxury of shopping in air-conditioned comfort.

Going Out

Introduction

Whether you decide to soak up some Arabic atmosphere, sample international cuisines or shimmy to world famous DJs – you're guaranteed a good night out in Bahrain.

As one of the more relaxed Gulf states, Bahrain boasts an impressive number of restaurants, bars and clubs, so visitors are often surprised by the quality of the nightlife. Each area has its own, distinct feel, from the neon sleaze of Hoora to the laidback vibe in Adliya, where the range of food on offer is quite staggering. See the Best For... table on page 124 for a quick and easy way to find what you fancy in your area. Venues are then arranged by area and divided into restaurants (with cuisine type listed), cafes, pubs, bars then nightclubs.

Much of the action takes place in the hotels and it's here you'll find top-class restaurants and old-fashioned pubs. Bear in mind that things don't get going until later on so don't book a table before 21:00 or you could be sitting on your own! A service charge of 15% is automatically added to the bill and you can add a 10% tip for your waiter if you were particularly impressed.

Alcohol can be quite expensive, but going out mid-week guarantees cheap prices and Friday brunches will often include unlimited booze. Walking isn't generally advised, simply because of the lack of footpaths, but Adliya has lots of restaurants, so it's ideal for a pre-dinner stroll in the cooler months.

Whatever your budget you can find a menu to suit, and the inexpensive array of Arabic and international choices make Bahrain the perfect place to try something new.

Best For...

If you're in a musical mood, fancy trying some local cuisine or just want to find the best place for a strong drink then check out the table below. Explorer's top picks in Bahrain have been handily compiled for your eating and drinking pleasure – maximum enjoyment with minimal effort.

Alfresco		
Bam Bu!	Manama City East	p.134
Kontiki Asia	Manama City Centre	p.128
La Fontaine	Manama City East	p.143
Seafood Hut	Best of the Rest	p.166
Trader Vic's	Manama City West	p.154
Breakfast		
Cafe Lilou	Manama City East	p.150
Cappuccino Cafe	North-West	p.162
Coco's	Manama City East	p.150
La Mosaique	Manama City Centre	p.128
Ric's Kountry Kitchen	Manama City East	p.147
THE One	Manama City West	p.156
Buffets		
Clipper Bar	Manama City Centre	p.131
La Mosaique	Manama City Centre	p.128
Lanterns	North-West	p.160
Neyran	Manama City West	p.152
Olivo's Brasserie	Manama City Centre	p.129
Silk's	Best of the Rest	p.164
Krumz	Manama City East	p.140
Upstairs Downstairs	Manama City East	p.147

Casual		
Chili's	Manama City West	p.152
Hash House	Manama City East	p.139
Jim's	Manama City East	p.140
Mamma Mia	Best of the Rest	p.164
Senor Paco's	Manama City East	p.147
Zytoun	Manama City East	p.149

Cocktails		
Burlington Club	Manama City West	p.157
Casa Bar	Manama City West	p.157
Rock Bottom Cafe	Manama City East	p.151
Trader Vic's	Manama City West	p.154

Kids Welcome		
Applebee's	Manama City West	p.152
Camelot	Manama City East	p.136
Casa Mexicana	Manama City East	p.137
Clay Oven	Manama City East	p.137
Ric's Kountry Kitchen	Manama City East	p.147

Live Music		
Lanterns	North-West	p.160
Mezzaluna	Manama City East	p.144
Mondo	Manama City Centre	p.129
Silk's	Best of the Rest	p.164
Senor Paco's	Manama City East	p.147

Local Cuisine		
Al Berdaouni	Manama City Centre	p.126
Al Sawani Restaurant	Manama City East	p.134
Layali Zaman	Manama City East	p.144

Reservations Recommended		
Hong Kong	North-West	p.158
Krumz	Manama City East	p.140
Monsoon	Manama City East	p.146
Plums	Manama City West	p.154
Upstairs Downstairs	Manama City East	p.147

Manama City Centre

From hot clubs to the best views in town, if you want a taste of luxury look beyond the skyscapers to some of the best hotels on the island.

Al Berdaouni
Arabic/Lebanese

Regency InterContinental, City Centre 1722 7777

An Arabian night comes alive when the entertainment starts at Al Berdaouni. Start by picking your way through the incredible array of hot and cold Lebanese mezze as the belly dancers come onto the stage. Authentic spices make the succulent meat and fish dishes mouth-wateringly tasty. Have a go with the dancers and shake up some room for dessert. Top off your night with some sweet tea and shisha. Map A 1

Asia
Far Eastern

City Centre Hotel, City Centre 1722 9979

Aesthetically stunning, the decor in Asia is wickedly chic and very sophisticated. Typically of Japanese food, the portions are on the small side, but tasty. A lovely light Thai lunch comes in at a mere BD 2 while the a la carte menu is extensive. The place gets busy when the DJ arrives. A dazzling selection of drinks is available from the well-stocked bar, so be adventurous. Map A 2

KEI
Japanese

Golden Tulip Hotel, Diplomatic Area 1753 5000

KEI offers a friendly welcome amid a cool, serene, mirrored interior. Taking centre stage is your chef who will entertain

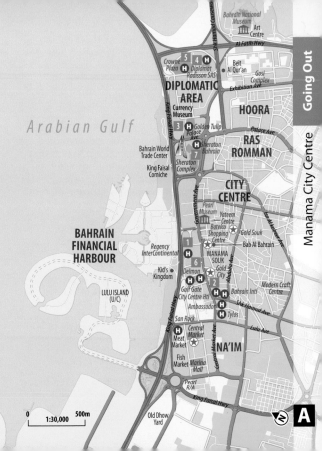

Bahrain National Museum

Art Centre

Shk Hamad Causeway

Al Fatih Hwy

Crowne Plaza **5**

Diplomat

Radisson SAS

Beit Al Qur'an

Gosi Complex

Exhibition Ave

DIPLOMATIC AREA

HOORA

Currency Museum

3 Golden Tulip

Palace Ave

Palace Ave

RAS ROMMAN

Shk Isa Hwy

Bahrain World Trade Center

Sheraton Bahrain **7**

King Faisal Corniche

Sheraton Complex

Arabian Gulf

CITY CENTRE

Government Ave

Pearl Museum

Yateem Centre

Batelco Shopping Centre

Gold Souk

Isa Al Kabeer Ave

1

Bab Al Bahrain

MANAMA SOUK

BAHRAIN FINANCIAL HARBOUR

Regency InterContinental

6 Delmon

Gold City **2**

Abdulla Ave

Kid's Kingdom

Golf Gate

City Centre Htl

Bahrain Intl

Modern Craft Centre

Ambassador

Shk Hamad Ave

San Rock

Tylos

LULU ISLAND (U/C)

King Faisal Hwy

Central Meat Market

Lulu Ave

NA'IM

Fish Market

Central Market Ave

Marina Mall

Pearl R/A

King Faisal Hwy

0   500m

1:30,000

Old Dhow Yard

A

by preparing your meal in full view. The choice is almost bewildering with a strong bias towards seafood. Quality, not quantity, is top priority. Meals are immaculately presented and are accompanied by heartwarming sake. Map A **3**

Kontiki Asia
Far Eastern
Diplomat Radisson SAS Hotel, Diplomatic Area   1752 5210

This restaurant, offering a great range of Far Eastern cuisine, is something of an enigma. Dine here on a busy evening and the atmosphere is vibrant but when Kontiki is empty, the mood deflates. Dine alfresco on a balmy evening and enjoy a specially prepared cocktail at the bar. If your timing is right, Kontiki can be an elegant choice for a meal out. Map A **4**

La Mosaique
International
Crowne Plaza Hotel, Diplomatic Area   1753 1122

La Mosaique offers a delightful introduction to Middle Eastern food. While the starters are more international in flavour, each entree is deliciously Arabic. The buffet is generous and readily replenished, while kebabs and lamb chops can be cooked in front of you and brought to your table. If you have room left for dessert, try the fine selection of cakes and puddings. In cooler months the outdoor terrace is great for alfresco dining with the added advantage of a sea view. Map A **5**

Marrakesh
Moroccan
Delmon International Hotel, City Centre   1722 4000

As with most Middle Eastern restaurants, it is probably best to go with a group of friends so a large selection of mezze can be shared. Desserts are very tempting and must be accompanied by the traditional Arabic coffee. Marrakesh is authentically decorated and the atmosphere is cosy and live entertainment, thanks to a traditional oud player and singer, serves as a pleasant background to dinner conversation. Weekends are wild so book well in advance to avoid disappointment. Map A 6

Mondo
Italian

Diplomat Radisson SAS Hotel, Diplomatic Area   1753 1666

Mondo is Italian chic at its best. A powerful use of colours in the restaurant's design is mirrored in the very impressive menu and you'll feel like you are dining at a rather upmarket Milanese restaurant. Expect to make your choice then change your mind a few times before finally deciding – everything sounds delicious! An excellent array of meat, pasta, fish and vegetarian entrees and mains fill the menu, and when you get your food it is very filling. Service here is friendly, relaxed and unpretentious. Despite its expensive appearance, there is nothing nouveau about Mondo's food and you might find yourself trying to justify the fairly high prices. Map A 4

Olivo's Brasserie
International

Diplomat Radisson SAS Hotel, Diplomatic Area   1758 4400

Expect to be spoilt for choice at the buffet; everything is beautifully displayed and fabulously tempting. A wide selection of food is on offer from French to Indian featuring delectable and unusual flavours. Time is clearly spent on the outstanding presentation and the staff are professional, efficient and on hand to look after you. The decor is tasteful

and Olivo's offers a very peaceful and enjoyable lunch away from the rush of the city. Map A **4**

Soie

Chinese

Sheraton Hotel, Diplomatic Area

1753 3533

Soie's staff warmly welcome diners to their cocoon of lush colours and the menu offers a tempting range of dishes. The choices are delicious and in general the food is of a very high standard. All in all, Soie is a very relaxing and enjoyable place you will want to revisit. Map A **7**

Versailles

French

Regency InterContinental, City Centre

1722 7777

This upmarket restaurant makes the perfect venue for romancing that special someone. Offering a mouth-watering selection of dishes, the French chef is joined once a month by a different Michelin star chef. The set menu is complemented by an impressive list of daily specials, and the extensive wine list is of the highest quality. In terms of decor, think tasteful, French, and most importantly, romantic. Map A **1**

Clipper Bar

Bar

Regency InterContinental, City Centre

1722 7777

This place is well known to locals and the international clientele who stay at the Regency. The choice of food is as varied as the beer and the Thursday lunch buffet is a good opportunity to try the much loved traditional roast for a mere BD 3.900. On regular nights the atmosphere is lively, so enjoy a few pints during happy hour and watch the band. Map A **1**

Fiddler's Green

Pub

Diplomat Radisson SAS Hotel, Diplomatic Area   1753 1666

This place is the quintessential London city boozer, rowdy
Irish country pub and upmarket hotel bar all rolled into one.
Not an easy combination but one achieved very successfully
by Fiddler's friendly management and staff who seamlessly
cater for expats, locals and visitors. There's a wide range of
beverages and the pub food includes home-cooked Irish
stew or delicious shepherd's pie, and don't miss the carvery
roast every night (except Friday) for BD 4 which includes a
free half-pint of lager. Map A ◢

Harvesters

Pub

Crowne Plaza Hotel, Diplomatic Area   1753 1122

Early in the evening, this is a typical hotel bar with small
groups of businessmen unwinding after a long day but
later a raucous Filipino rock band transforms the sleepy
bar with scantily-clad dancers and toe-tapping numbers.
There is an extensive cocktail list and a different drinks
promotion every night of the week (except Thursdays)
including free drinks for ladies on Mondays and super
cheap pitchers of beer on Wednesdays. The food is served
in ample portions and is of a standard that you would
expect from a top-class joint. Map A ◢

Al Nada

Bar

Sheraton Hotel, Diplomatic Area   1753 3533

An Nada is a popular spot for both business people and
hotel guests to wind down after a busy day in the

boardroom or exploring Bahrain. The modern setting attracts a mix of nationalities that come to play pool and darts as well as enjoy the long happy hour, which runs from 13:00 to 21:00, while the house band keeps things lively with covers of all the favourites. Map A 7

Diggers   Pub
Delmon International Hotel, City Centre   1722 4000

One of older bars on the island, Diggers is an undemanding pub with few concessions to modern fashions. If you want a wholesome steak and a few beers then Diggers is just the place. The food is very reasonably priced and the ample portions will help soak up the wide variety of beer available. With massive TV screens showing big games from all over the world, the longest happy hour in Bahrain (noon to 21:00) and regular dinner specials, this place is a real hit with western males. Map A 6

Likwid   Nightclub
City Centre Hotel, City Centre   1771 6062

Likwid is an intimate venue with clean, cool and modern decor. Regular and guest DJs play at Likwid on Wednesdays, Thursdays and Fridays but it also comes into its own on Monday nights when the hot salsa band, La Movida, takes the floor. From 20:00 you can learn the salsa steps and at 21:30, you can practice your moves. Likwid also has a private room behind the main club that is open on Wednesdays for wine-tasting. For BD 2.500 you can try six different wines (repeatedly) and sample from trays of nibbles. Map A 2

Manama City East

Food fans will be in heaven in this part of town with everything from BD 1 shawarmas to sophisticated cuisine from all over the world.

Al Sawani Restaurant
Arabic/Lebanese
Nr Marina Club, Hoora
1729 7333

Enter Al Sawani and step into a world of chic and simple sophistication; this is Bahraini decor at its finest. A calm, quiet and unhurried atmosphere pervades until the lights are dimmed and the nightly live entertainment begins. A sumptuous array of authentic Lebanese and Bahraini dishes awaits and they are well worth waiting for. Portions are a good size, beautifully presented and tasty. Map B **1**

Bam Bu!
Chinese
Off Osama Bin Zaid Avenue, Adliya
1771 4424

This restaurant is excellent value for money and especially popular for groups. Drink and eat as much as you like for BD 12 or you can order a set menu and as the dishes arrive just ask the waiters to replenish your favourites. The food is Asian fusion and boasts a tantalising menu of classic favourites, as well as a taste of something a little more unique. Map B **2**

Beijing
Chinese
Off Osama Bin Zaid Avenue, Adliya
1771 7969

You can't miss Beijing's huge red lanterns hanging at the entrance gates – red denotes good luck in Chinese and this

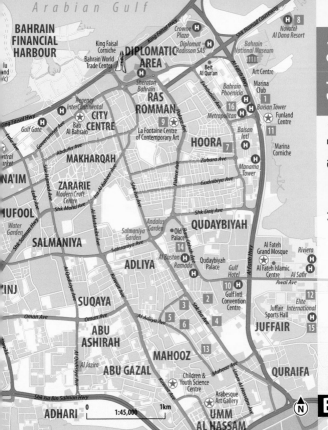

Arabian Gulf

BAHRAIN
FINANCIAL
HARBOUR

King Faisal Corniche
Bahrain World
Trade Center

Crowne
Plaza

Diplomat
Radisson SAS

Shk Hamad Causeway

8 Novotel
Al Dana Resort

DIPLOMATIC
AREA

Bahrain
National Museum

Sheraton
Bahrain

Beit
Al Qur'an

Art Centre

RAS
ROMMAN

Regency
InterContinental

Bab
Al Bahrain

CITY
CENTRE

Gulf Gate

King Faisal Hwy

Government Ave

Abdulla Ave

MAKHARQAH

 central
market

NA'IM

ZARARIE
Modern Craft
Centre
Shk Mohd Ave

MUFOOL

Water
Garden

SALMANIYA

'INJ

SUQAYA

ABU
ASHIRAH

9

La Fontaine Centre
of Contemporary Art

Exhibition Ave

Palace Ave

Bahrain
Phoenicia

Metropolitan

Marina
Club

1

16

Baisan Tower
Funland
Centre

HOORA

7

Prince Ave

Zabara Ave

Gudaibiyah Ave

Baisan
Intl

11

Marina
Corniche

Manama
Tower

Shk Daij Ave

Andalus
Garden

Salmaniya
Garden

Al Khalifa Ave

Salmaniya Ave

QUDAYBIYAH

Old
Palace

14

Al Bustan
Ramada

Qudaibiyah
Palace

Al Fateh
Grand Mosque

Riviera

Al Fateh Islamic
Centre

Al Safir

Awal Ave

ADLIYA

Shk Hamad Ave

Al Qudaibiya Ave

Oman Ave

Oman Ave

ABU
GAZAL

Al Jazira

3

Al Adliya Ave

5

6

Shk Isa Ave

Gulf
Hotel

2

13

10 Gulf Intl
Convention
Centre

4

Al Fateh Hwy

Juffair
International
Sports Hall

Elite
International

12

JUFFAIR

15

MAHOOZ

Children &
Youth Science
Centre

Mahooz Ave

QURAIFA

Arabesque
Art Gallery

Shk Isa Bin Salman Hwy

ADHARI

0

1:45,000

1km

UMM
AL HASSAM

N

B

simple little restaurant is a fortunate find. The prices are ridiculously low with most appetisers starting at around BD 1 and mains around BD 3. The portions are ample and all the accompanying sauces are imported from the owner's hometown of Shanghai. A great place for a cheap and cheerful introduction to Chinese cuisine. Map B **2**

Caesar's
Shk Isa Avenue, Adliya

International
1771 6955

This restaurant embodies elegant dining, and the term 'fusion' permeates through everything here, from the decor to the cuisine, an eclectic mix of Chinese, Indian and European. Tasty, piping hot and extremely filling, almost everything on the menu is worth trying, especially the fresh, crispy spring rolls. The waiters are extremely helpful and always on hand to advise. An international clientele frequent Caesar's and reservations are essential at weekends. Map B **3**

Camelot
Off Shk Isa Avenue, Adliya

International
1771 7745

You can't miss this pseudo-medieval castle rising up from the surrounding Bahraini villas. The medieval theme continues inside, but forget the roast hog on a spit, instead it's all sofas in quiet corners and outside dining by the moat. The menu includes lots of vegetarian options as well as steak, fish and pork. With an Irish manager at the helm, you'll see his influence with full Irish breakfast including black pudding on the menu. Map B **4**

Casa Mexicana
Off Al Adliya Avenue, Adliya

Mexican
1771 5521

This Mexican restaurant guarantees its customers an authentic funfest. Magnificent margaritas flow all night as you tuck in to the huge portions of hot and spicy meals, and if you're still up to it, finish off with traditional tequilas. The dancefloor can get quite hot and spicy too as the night draws to an end. This light-hearted restaurant, with Mexican memorabilia on its walls, will keep you and your guests smiling all night. Map B 5

Clay Oven
Off Al Adliya Avenue, Adliya

Indian
1771 7008

It is hard to find fault with this homely, yet rather elegant, restaurant that serves exquisite Indian food. The tandoori items are indeed cooked in a traditional clay oven (tandoor), and you can tell. Children are welcomed and amply catered for. What sets this restaurant apart is their care of customers. Stuck for a lift? They might even arrange to pick you up. Other items of interest include an old swing seat and a traditional hut in the garden selling old Indian wares to keep you occupied between courses. Map B 6

Bohemia
Off Osama Bin Zaid Avenue, Adliya

French
1771 6715

Bohemia is worth a visit for its decor alone. Downstairs you'll find a cafe in deep tones with a tribute to Marilyn Monroe and a lounge bar in Salvador Dali style – all purples and greens, mirrored ceilings and lip-shaped

settees. Upstairs is for formal dining; the textured walls and ambient lighting give the main dining hall a funky flavour. The cafe serves sandwiches, salads, pastas and curries, while the upstairs restaurant goes for Mediterranean dishes with fish aplenty. Map B 2

Hard Rock Café
Exhibition Avenue, Hoora

American
1729 1569

The interior of this American chain is a real treat; walls covered with movie memorabilia, guitars, jackets, signed photos, gold albums and much more. Kids are welcome and are provided with fun drawing activities, while hungry grown-ups peruse the extensive menu. American favourites and Tex-Mex combinations feature highly with huge portions (staff will provide a doggy-bag at the end of the meal). The kids' menu is reasonable and will keep them satisfied until the inevitable request for dessert. Map B 7

Hash House
Off Osama Bin Zaid Avenue, Adliya

Thai
1771 5775

From the moment you sit down until the moment you have to leave, you will feel looked after, spoilt and fully satisfied over a dinner that easily turns into a wonderful experience. The famous papaya salad is a definite must-try, along with the yummy starters, but be careful to save room for the huge choice of Thai main courses available on the menu. This place has great warmth to it – so if you are looking for a Thai experience, you've come to the right place. Map B 2

La Fontaine

Jean-Pierre Cohen

Dinner Cruise

Novotel Al Dana Resort, Off Shk Hamad Causeway   3909 4382

These traditional dhow cruises depart for the daytime cruise at 09:15 and head to the nearby islands. Sit back and enjoy a Turkish brunch of barbecue meats, fresh salads and plenty of refreshments. Evening cruises depart at 18:00, touring the coastline and stopping at some smaller islands. Map B 8

Jim's

International

Off Osama Bin Zaid Avenue, Adliya   1771 0654

Knock on the heavy wooden door and the staff will usher you in. Wicker chairs with over-stuffed cushions create a homely atmosphere in this very popular eatery. This restaurant offers all the traditional English comfort food you would expect and more. Portions are fantastic, and you'll be hard pushed to clean your plate. Jim's is quiet and romantic on weekdays, and fun-filled at weekends. Map B 2

Krumz

European

Off Osama Bin Zaid Avenue, Adliya   1771 2767

The dishes available at Krumz are delicious, richly flavoured and generous in size. It has an extensive menu with plenty of variety and there is an early bird menu that includes unlimited quantities of wine and draught beers. You'll find the atmosphere casual and congenial. The restaurant has been awarded Le Plat D'Argent twice for its superb service and the Friday brunch is particularly popular. Map B 2

Mezzaluna

La Cave
European
Off Osama Bin Zaid Avenue, Adliya · 1771 7705

This place combines a little bit of everything; succulent steak, the freshest salads, delicious side dishes, to-die-for chocolate brownies and as much vino as you can drink. La Cave's speciality is their set menu; you get three choices of salad, a choice of meat, fish or chicken and three options for dessert. The staff and service are irreproachable; add this to the chic ambience and it's an excellent choice. Map B **2**

La Fontaine Centre of Contemporary Art
French
92 Hoora Avenue, Hoora · 1723 0123

This spectacular old Bahraini monument has been lovingly restored to include a spa, art gallery and Pilates studio. The restaurant is situated in the main courtyard with a titanic-sized fountain in the middle. Quiet during the day, the place really comes into its own for parties and events including film screenings. The food in the restaurant is of a very high standard and covers a spectrum of cuisines. Map B **9**

La Perle
French
Novotel Al Dana Resort, Off Shk Hamad Causeway · 1729 8439

This unique restaurant's location provides a stunning ocean backdrop from almost every table. Delicious lobster, hammour and other seafood delights are served on huge blue and white plates and the colour scheme, in keeping with the coastal location, is continued throughout the restaurant. La Bellevue Bar upstairs entertains guests with a lively Latin American band in a comfortable atmosphere. Map B **8**

La Perle

La Pergola

Gulf Hotel, Adliya

Italian

1771 3000

Less of a traditional trattoria and more like a five-star fine dining establishment, La Pergola pleases Italian food lovers as well as sophisticated diners. The menu is packed with all the usual suspects, as well as a few surprises and of particular note are the desserts. One thing everything has in common is quality; of flavours, presentation, and delivery. All in all, this is one of Bahrain's most distinguished Italians. Map B 10

Layali Zaman

Next to Funland, Al Fatih Highway, Hoora

Arabic/Lebanese

1729 3097

Situated on the corniche, this is a quiet retreat from the neon noise of Funland next door. Delightfully ramshackle, you can tuck into a cheap and cheerful meal here or puff on a shisha while you sip your fruit juice. The sea view and ample parking make it a relaxing and convenient spot to sample the unpretentious fare of sandwiches, salads and delicious grills. Map B 11

Mezzaluna

Off Osama Bin Zaid Avenue, Adliya

International

1774 2999

This restaurant is an authentic old Bahraini house with a covered courtyard. The lighting is low, the waiters attentive and the general atmosphere is conducive to good times. Expect to find timeless classics such as steak, as well as more adventurous dishes and one of the most extensive wine lists on the island. With a grand piano and jazz quartet on Fridays, this restaurant is perfect for a special evening out. Map B 2

Monsoon

Mirai
Japanese

Off Osama Bin Zaid Avenue, Adliya
1771 3113

Mirai is, without a doubt, one of Bahrain's most sophisticated restaurants. The sushi chef is also the restaurant's manager and he is truly loyal to the art of Japanese cuisine. The restaurant has a wonderful ambience created by the sleek, modern, minimalist decor. The menu offers plenty of choice and DJs add to this hip experience with the latest mixes from the Middle East. Map B 2

Monsoon
Far Eastern

Off Osama Bin Zaid Avenue, Adliya
1774 9222

Monsoon is an impressive establishment; the decor inspired by a Balinese palace, with a raised central dining area and water features. There is a clever blend of Asian food with a comprehensive selection of Japanese fare. The presentation, quality and taste of everything is superb. It's the perfect place for a special meal. Map B 2

Oliveto
Italian

Shk Isa Avenue, Adliya
1771 6747

The wine list is more than substantial, with expensive as well as sensibly priced wines available by the glass or bottle. Traditional Italian dishes such as the brilliant saltimboca alla romana, an appetiser with veal, are hard to beat, and the equally authentic desserts including tiramisu and casatta are superbly presented and flavoursome. You might even get an Italian liqueur on the house. Map B 4

Ric's Kountry Kitchen
Shabab Avenue, Juffair

American
1772 5550

This restaurant is as close as you will get to a home-made American meal; everything from grits to blueberry pancakes feature on the menu. This place will cure any home-sickness for mom's cooking and the rest of us can appreciate finger-lickingly good comfort food. There is also a lively bar where the staff keep customers smiling, so it's a good starting point for a night out. Map B 12

Senor Paco's
Al Adliya Avenue, Adliya

Mexican
1772 5873

Senor Paco's is packed to the oak rafters most nights. Fajitas, steaks, vegetarian options and all the Mexican trimmings are served up but don't expect to stick to a low calorie or carb diet here – the free nachos and dip don't help! Margarita night on Fridays always pulls in a big crowd, creating a fun atmosphere with live music and plenty of partying. Map B 13

Upstairs Downstairs
Nr British School, Adliya

International
1771 3093

Upstairs Downstairs is on everyone's list of favourites; a smart dining area upstairs with a relaxed, informal lounge area downstairs. Ingeniously done up, the restaurant serves international cuisine and resembles a cosy jazz club with a dash of Georgian London. A jazz musician keeps the atmosphere buzzing and international artists fly in to perform at a monthly 'Friday Night Live' so keep an eye on event listings to see who could be serenading you. Map B 6

Zoë
Off Osama Bin Zaid Avenue, Adliya

International
1771 6400

Easy to find, this place is both chic and unique. The menu offers a wide range of food with pastas and pizzas, seafood and steaks, and the fresh-baked breads are to die for. For lunch it is quiet and pleasant, while in the evenings it is more convivial. Its formal yet relaxed undertones make it an ideal place to eat with friends or family. Map B 2

Zytoun
Novotel Al Dana Resort, Shk Hamad Causeway

Mediterranean
1729 8008

Located at the Novotel Al Dana Resort, Zytoun offers an alfresco poolside dining area, leading down to the beach. The Mediterranean-style food is reasonably priced, delicious and creatively presented. Zytoun has daily buffets at every meal and a la carte is also available. The theme nights are popular. Thoughtfully, the restaurant keeps a children's table with activities and toys to keep the little ones happy. Map B 8

Al Bareh
Off Shk Isa Avenue, Adliya

Cafe
1771 3535

An absolute haven of tranquility and culture tucked away in a picturesque old house, Al Bareh serves a selection of superb Arabic fusion cuisine encompassing many healthy and low-carb delights. The other feature is a modern art gallery upstairs featuring big names in Middle Eastern art. Menu prices are reasonable and the charming outdoor terrace is an ideal spot for a light lunch in winter. Map B 4

Zoë

Café Lilou
Cafe

Off Osama Bin Zaid Avenue, Adliya
1771 4440

Café Lilou is all decadence and old Parisian romance. It is primarily known for its delectable cakes, afternoon teas and breakfast menu. Top choices include the scrambled eggs, mini burgers and outstanding juices. Whether you're dropping by for lunch or dinner, the menu shifts for bigger, more exotic choices, still healthy and still very glamorous. Map B **2**

Coco's
Cafe

Off Osama Bin Zaid Avenue, Adliya
1771 6512

This popular spot offers rustic decor and continental cuisine in huge portions. The food is reliably good, the prices are fair and the iced tea is superb. During the day this is a great choice for a late breakfast or a light lunch and in the evenings the courtyard is a perfect meeting place. Map B **2**

La Ventana
Cafe

Off Osama Bin Zaid Avenue, Adliya
1771 6771

La Ventana's home-made and freshly-prepared food is its main attraction and it is famed for its fantastic salads. Stuffed baguettes, baked potatoes and hearty soups are the makings of this buzzing cafe. While you eat, sit and admire the works of local artists displayed on the walls. Map B **2**

JJ's Irish Pub
Pub

Al Bustan Hotel, Adliya
1774 2323

This is undoubtedly one of the best bars on the island. Popular and busy, it boasts a genuinely mixed crowd of all nationalities and age groups. Downstairs has a lengthy bar and modest dancing space, while upstairs has its own smaller bar and a few pool tables. The food is decent and there are drink offers or theme nights every day. Map B 14

Rock Bottom Café
Ramee International, Juffair

Bar
1772 7230

This American-themed bar is a lively venue offering a good selection of food, drink deals and western-style entertainment. There's plenty of space, pool tables and big eats on the menu. The band keeps the party going every night except Mondays and the bar is open till 02:00. Map B 15

BJ's
Nr Al Bustan Hotel, Adliya

Nightclub
1771 6062

BJ's is the closest you'll find to a western-style nightclub and there is normally a good crowd. Leaning on the cheesy side, the dancefloor is a fair size, and there's sultry red feel thanks to both the decor and lighting. Upstairs is another bar, with velvet sofas and a gallery overlooking the dancefloor. Map B 14

F1
Metropolitan Hotel, Hoora

Nightclub
1729 6464

Perched on the edge of the entertainment strip of Exhibition Avenue, F1 is a busy westerner's nightspot. At weekends the thirsty crowd can make it hard to reach either of the two well-stocked bars and big-game nights draw all age-groups. International food is available for reasonable prices. Map B 16

Manama City West

Go west to fill up on hearty grub before shopping, hit a pool party or luxuriate in the splendour of world-class hotels.

Applebee's
Nxt Bahrain Mall, Sanabis

American
1755 2834

This lively, international Tex-Mex chain has a refreshingly modern decor, and is well-stocked with young couples, singles and families. The menu is packed with favourites guaranteed to leave you feeling well and truly satisfied and the free soft drink refills are all part of the excellent service. Arrive hungry and wear loose clothing! Map C 1

Chili's
Nxt Seef Mall, Seef

American
1758 1221

Although this big Tex-Mex chain has a somewhat generic menu, it offers high quality food. Dieters need not worry; one of Chili's strong points is an excellent 'guiltless' menu that gives delicious low-fat and low-carb options. Chili's is also a winner for families and Thursday lunchtimes especially are child friendly with entertainers, including a magician who also conjures on Friday. Map C 2

Neyran
Mercure Grand Hotel, Seef

International
1758 4400

As yet undiscovered by the masses, Neyran is a real treat. The lunch buffet is quite extraordinary with lobster thermidor and beef in veal liver gravy. It's not just fancy cuisine though;

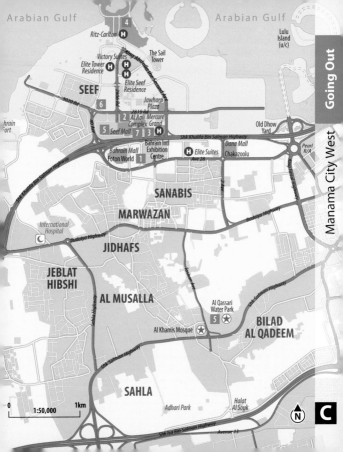

Arabian Gulf

Arabian Gulf

Lulu Island
(u/c)

Ritz-Carlton

The Sail
Tower

Victory Suites

Elite Tower
Residence

Elite Seef
Residence

SEEF

6

Jawhara
Plaza

2819 Rd

Al Aali
Complex

Mercure
Grand

5 Seef Mall

7 3

Old Dhow
Yard

Shk Khalifa Bin Salman Highway

Pearl
R/A

Bahrain Mall
Foton World

1

Bahrain Intl
Exhibition
Centre

Elite Suites

Ave 28

Dana Mall

Chakazoolu

rain
rt

3020 Rd

Shk Khalifa Bin Salman Highway

SANABIS

MARWAZAN

International
Hospital

Budaiya Highway

Budaiya Highway

JIDHAFS

**JEBLAT
HIBSHI**

AL MUSALLA

Al Qassari
Water Park

5

Al Khamis Mosque

**BILAD
AL QADEEM**

Sahla Highway

Shk Salman Highway

Shk Salman Highway

Route Ave

SAHLA

Adhari Park

Halat
Al Souk

Shk Isa Bin Salman Highway

Avenue 13

0   1:50,000   1km

N

C

Indian, Arabic and Italian dishes are all here too. The service is attentive, while the atmosphere is quiet – aided by the extensive drinks menu. This is an ideal place for a business lunch or a special dinner. Map C 3

Plums
International

The Ritz-Carlton, Bahrain Hotel & Spa, Seef

1758 0000

With its deep purple walls, velvet seating and sensual lighting, this is the perfect setting for a romantic dinner. The appetisers are phenomenal, but it's the sumptuous steaks that are the speciality. The food is beautifully presented, but make sure you bring something warm as the air conditioning reaches Arctic temperatures. Map C 4

Primavera
Italian

The Ritz-Carlton, Bahrain Hotel & Spa, Seef

1758 0000

No matter what you eat, any place that offers a picturesque beach backdrop is worth a visit. Expect the staff to politely assist you throughout your meal and the head chef visits each table. An extensive wine list accompanies the noveau cuisine menu that lists freshly made pastas and breads, while the set menu offers some innovative choices. Map C 4

Trader Vic's
Polynesian

The Ritz-Carlton, Bahrain Hotel & Spa, Seef

1758 6555

Trader Vic's is as much a restaurant as it is a bar. It sports trendy Polynesian decor and views over the beach. You can linger over a delicious Asian-inspired meal, or munch your way through crispy wontons and other oriental finger foods,

Plums

or even just savour a few of their famously exotic cocktails. The wide selection of inventive and artistic drinks adds to the holiday feel provided by the sultry Cuban band. Map C **4**

Aroma Café
Seef Mall, Seef

Cafe
1725 2343

Hidden in the heart of Seef Mall, the true spirit of this coffee shop is Arabic, with unobtrusive Arabic music and mainly local clientele, but there is an Italian focus to the menu. Prices are decent, portions are substantial and the presentation is impeccable. This interesting spot is a unique retreat. Map C **5**

Le Chocolat
Nr Seef Mall, Seef

Cafe
1758 2259

Le Chocolat is light and airy and the open patio is pleasant during the cooler winter months. The cafe is well known for delicious European chocolates, all elegantly gift-wrapped, while the menu offers a fine selection of cakes and pastas, sandwiches, soups and light main courses. The presentation is excellent and portions are good, as are the prices. Map C **6**

THE One
Al Aali Shopping Complex, Seef

Cafe
1758 7178

This upmarket cafe, attached to the homeware shop, is the perfect place for daytime dining and an excellent alternative venue for an early evening meal. There are some classic salads and sandwiches as well as more adventurous items such as chicken with spiced chocolate sauce. Efficient staff and healthy kids' menu round off this excellent eatery. Map C **7**

The Lobby Lounge
Afternoon Tea

The Ritz-Carlton, Bahrain Hotel & Spa, Seef · 1758 0000

Nestled beneath the vast atrium of the Ritz-Carlton Hotel lies The Lobby Lounge where guests can sip afternoon tea while being serenaded by a string quartet. Alternatively, come for an elegant working buffet breakfast, or order one of the flavoured frappucinos and a cake freshly baked and displayed in the patisserie across the lobby. Map C 4

Burlington Club
Bar

The Ritz-Carlton, Bahrain Hotel & Spa, Seef · 1758 0000

The Burlington Club is an intimate, comfortable and stylish venue offering a selection of innovative cocktails using the highest quality of ingredients. With leather sofas and winged chairs, it recreates a typical 'gentleman's club,' although one where ladies are very welcome. The Cigar Room boasts choices that will satisfy the tastes of the pickiest of aficionados, who often stay to hear the lively band that kicks in from 20:30. Map C 4

Casa Bar
Bar

Mercure Grand Hotel, Seef · 1758 7400

This plush nightspot is discreetly tucked away on the first floor of the Mercure Grand hotel. It's a sumptuous bar decorated in modern Arabic style where you can enjoy a happy hour from 18:00 to 20:00 every day. Upmarket pub grub is available at all times except on Fridays, when you can enjoy an impressive buffet inclusive of all the sparking wine you can consume. Map C 3

North-West Bahrain

A short drive out of the capital will take you to some great family restaurants and some local favourites.

Anatolia
Turkish

Cypress Gardens, Budaiya Highway, Jannusan   1769 0601

Situated in Cypress Gardens, Anatolia's residential location is one of its selling points. The pleasant and charming villa atmosphere renders a Turkish feel throughout. Choose from a large number of well-priced starters and follow up with something from the extensive choice of grilled meats. Map D **1**

Cantina Spanish Court
International

Cypress Gardens, Budaiya Highway, Jannusan   1769 7552

Benoit Ducray, owner of the award-winning The Tipsy Lobster in Mauritius, has brought his love of fine cuisine to Bahrain. The interior has low-walled dining areas, hacienda-style seating and a dancefloor. The menu is updated every few months and is complemented by the extensive wine list. Ingredients include tuna from Japan and salmon from Norway, while breads and desserts are baked on demand. Map D **2**

Hong Kong
Chinese

Budaiya Highway, Jannusan   1772 8700

This restaurant opened in 1978 and quickly established an enviable reputation for its fine Chinese cuisine. Since then, they have increased in popularity, winning numerous awards and it is absolutely essential to book in advance. Once inside,

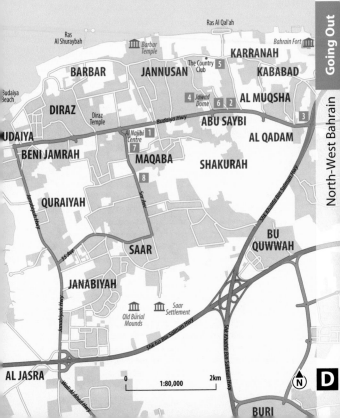

Arabian Gulf

Ras Al Shuraybah

Ras Al Qal'ah

Bahrain Fort

🏛 Barbar Temple

BARBAR

JANNUSAN

The Country Club **5**

KARRANAH

KABABAD

Budaiya Beach

DIRAZ

Diraz Temple

4 Jawad Dome

6 **2** AL MUQSHA

ABU SAYBI

3

UDAIYA

Al Najibi Centre **1**

Budaiya Hwy

AL QADAM

BENI JAMRAH

MAQABA

7

SHAKURAH

8

QURAIYAH

Saar Ave

Janabiyah Hwy

BU QUWWAH

SAAR

35 Ave

JANABIYAH

🏛 Old Burial Mounds

🏛 Saar Settlement

Sh. Isa Bin Salman Hwy

Sh. Khalifa Bin Salman Hwy

AL JASRA

Wadi Al Abd Hwy

0   1:80,000   2km

N

D

BURI

you'll see chefs create delicious meals using fresh produce flown in especially from various regions of China. Map D **2**

Lanterns
Indian

Off Budaiya Highway R/A, Al Muqsha
1759 0591

Suitable for every occasion, this restaurant is ideal for authentic Indian food. The setting is charming with traditional decor, unobtrusive live music and little dining kiosks. The all-you-can-eat-from-the-menu on Saturdays and the buffet on Mondays are great value. Lanterns is a fail-safe option and is one of the few establishments in the area serving alcohol. Map D **3**

Luigi's
Italian

Cypress Gardens, Budaiya Highway, Jannusan
1769 3533

Luigi's is a family-run pizzeria, and the proprietor and his charming wife take their pizzas very seriously indeed. All the ingredients are fabulously fresh, so it's little wonder this place is considered to serve the best pizza on the island. The tantalisingly thin crust and interesting toppings taste authentic, and the generous salads include delicious grilled cheese and rocket. The decor is rustic and the walls are adorned with cityscapes of Italian metropolises for a truly European experience. Map D **2**

Magic Wok
Chinese

Jawad Dome, Off Budaiya Highway, Jannusan
1769 4105

This fastfood joint has an impressively varied Asian menu that you wouldn't expect from a chain. Noodles and all-in-one stir-fries are specialities and the chef cooks your stir-fry in front of you, to your specifications, with no MSG added. It may not be haute cuisine, but the woks are constantly flipping fresh ingredients and the meals are always piping hot, tasty and filling. Map D 4

Brenigan's
Country Club, Jannusan

American
1759 3593

With consistently good food, Brenigan's is one of the few eateries in this area. It offers an excellent English-style bar with an impressive selection of beer on tap and pool tables for the energetic. Brenigan's has a picturesque tropical garden and during the cooler months it is one of the most romantic outdoor dining venues on the island. Map D 5

Chaing Saen
Cyprus Gardens, Budaiya Highway, Jannusan

Far Eastern
1759 2105

The food is delicious, and despite the large selection of dishes, it seems impossible to choose badly. There are three main options: Thai, Chinese and Japanese, all of which are cooked to order, full of flavour and as close to authentic as you'll get in Bahrain. The staff are extremely efficient (in a discreet kind of way), and any night of the week you come here you won't be disappointed. Map D 2

Lanna Thai
Budaiya Highway, Jannusan

Thai
1759 3940

Don't be deceived by Lanna Thai's appearance outside. Upstairs is fairly unremarkable but the downstairs dining area transports you to an elegant and cosy Thai-style haven with wood panels, sunken seating and comfy cushions. The menu offers a wide selection of appetisers, staples and fail-safe green and red Thai curries cooked to your required spiciness. Map D 6

Al Osra
Cafe

Al Najibi Centre, Budaiya Highway, Saar   1769 7558

Buzzing from 08:00 till the sun goes down, this little coffee shop is smack bang in the centre of one of the handiest shopping centres in Saar. Known as 'the goldfish bowl', you can't beat it for a quick snack and a lengthy chat. The menu is limited and the fare is standard, but is served by friendly staff and there's lots of free parking outside. Map D 7

Cappuccino Café
Cafe

Nr Al Najibi Centre, Off Budaiya Highway, Saar   1779 0404

Cappuccino Café is a little haven in Saar, away from the rush of the many other coffee shops in the area. With a focus on light breakfasts, quick bites and elegantly presented snacks, this reasonably priced coffee shop is a step above the rest. You won't be overwhelmed with the range of options on the menu, but for a leisurely rendezvous, Cappuccino Café is ideal. Map D 8

Delifrance
Cafe

Jawad Dome, Off Budaiya Highway, Jannusan   1769 6031

Crammed in the (often hectic) foodcourt of the popular Budaiya-based mini-mall, Jawad Dome, Delifrance bakes some of the island's most exquisite cakes and breads. All day breakfasts, light snacks, healthy soups and sandwiches are also on the menu, which you can eat in or take away. Map D 4

Best Of The Rest

Away from the usual haunts, take your time to explore the rest of Bahrain. You won't be disappointed.

BAPCO Club Restaurant
International
BAPCO Club, Awali
1775 3377

Located in Awali, a 30 minute drive from Manama, this is one of the quietest restaurants in Bahrain, but undeservedly so. Serving up first-rate food and with excellent service, it really should be full of patrons. Saturday is 'Seafood Night', with the popular grilled hammour, while Wednesday is 'Indian Thali Evening'. Map E **1**

Mamma Mia
Italian
Al Muaskar Highway Crossing, Riffa
1777 2321

Mamma Mia is said to be one of the best Italians on the island. This is not a fine dining restaurant but it is wonderfully cosy, offering an authentic feel with red-checked table cloths, low lighting and a warm welcome. You'll find traditional cooking with garlicky starters and superb home-made pastas and pizzas at excellent prices. Map E **2**

Silk's
International
Mövenpick Hotel, Muharraq
1746 0000

Renowned for its Monday night seafood buffet and excellent location next to the airport, this place is always bustling. Serving perhaps the freshest sushi in town, Silk's also offers you a choice of hammour, clams, squid, prawns and more,

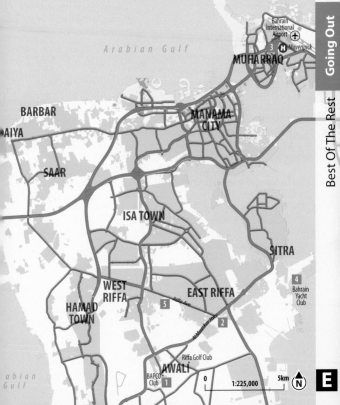

Arabian Gulf

Bahrain
International
Airport

Mövenpick

3

MUHARRAQ

**MANAMA
CITY**

BARBAR

AIYA

SAAR

ISA TOWN

SITRA

4
Bahrain
Yacht
Club

**WEST
RIFFA**

EAST RIFFA

5 *Riffa Ave*

**HAMAD
TOWN**

Al Manama Hwy

2

Riffa Golf Club

AWALI

BAPCO
Club

1

*abian
Gulf*

0   1:225,000   5km

N

cooked to your preference, but leave space for the tasty desserts. Enjoy the international ambience in the well-lit and airy environment with a beautiful garden view. Map E 3

Seafood Hut
Bahrain Yacht Club, Sitra

Seafood
1770 0677

The Seafood Hut at the Bahrain Yacht Club is hard to find, but it's well worth the hunt. Seafood is the order of the day with a menu ranging from impressive lobster dishes to the tried-and-trusted fish and chips. The service is warm, knowledgeable and always at hand. Map E 4

A Piece of Cake
Off Riffa Avenue, Riffa

Cafe
1759 6055

This delightful little coffee shop takes a modern Arabic approach to the decor and you will find watercolours of local scenes on the walls. Fresh and home-made sums up the fare; including light healthy snacks, scrumptious gateaux, croissants baked to order and eggs scrambled to creamy perfection. Map E 5

Flamingo Bar
Mövenpick Hotel, Muharraq

Bar
1746 0000

This is an excellent lounge for a few drinks and every night has special deals so you'll always find this place busy. Bar snacks are available for the peckish, and Silk's restaurant is next door for some stomach lining. The soft couches or standing bar area are well served by the bar staff and a band plays popular hits to entertain the international clientele. Map E 3

Silk's

Profile

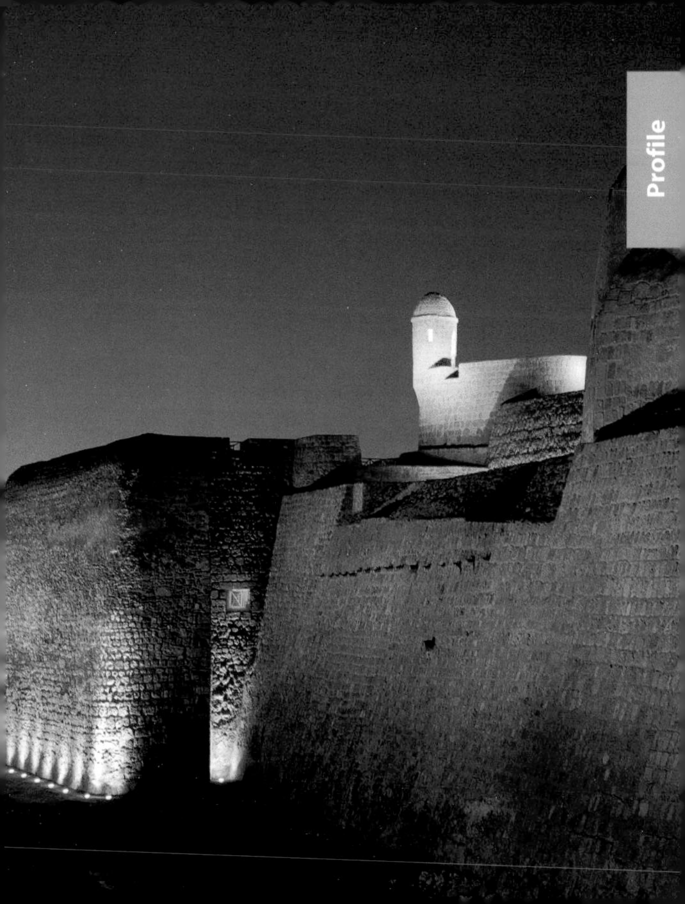

Culture

Bahrain may be bursting at the seams with development and growth, but that's taken nothing away from the country's splendid and unique culture.

In Bahraini culture, hospitality and courtesy are prized and visitors are often charmed by the friendliness of the people. Over the last 35 years, however, Bahrain has undergone rapid economic development, changing daily life considerably. People now seem a lot more hurried and less relaxed than they were a few years ago. Traditional pastimes have given way to more modern and universally practised activities, but Bahrainis can be proud of the ability to retain their essence while moving with the times.

Religion & Ramadan

Islam is the official religion of Bahrain, and is practised by 85% of the population. The majority of the Bahraini population (about 75%) are followers of the Shia sect, but the ruling family are Sunni. Freedom of worship is permitted to other faiths including Christianity, Hinduism, Parseeism, Judaism and Buddhism.

There are five main pillars of Islam, to which all followers must adhere: the testimony of faith, prayer, charity, fasting during the holy month of Ramadan and performing the Hajj pilgrimage at least once in a lifetime. Friday is Islam's holy day and is now the first day of most people's weekend.

The month of Ramadan is considered to be a holy month for Muslims, as it marks the period in which the

Holy Quran was revealed to Prophet Mohammed. The beginning of the month is marked by the sighting of the new moon, confirmed by a judiciary panel. During Ramadan, Muslims are expected to strive to a higher level of spirituality, and this is done in part by fasting during daylight hours. In the evening, the fast is broken with the Iftar meal. In Bahrain, working hours during Ramadan are shortened to six hours a day for Muslims. Some organisations extend this to non-Muslims too, who are also cautioned that it is illegal to eat, drink or smoke in public places during daylight hours, as a sign of respect to those who are fasting. The Ramadan timings can be found in local newspapers.

In practice, Ramadan is a time where all official business slows down considerably. However, the upside is that there is a celebratory atmosphere throughout the country every evening for a month.

In the villages, Bahrainis distribute dishes between houses most evenings for Iftar (breaking the fast) and Ghabgas (the late night meal and social gathering). Mosques are full for evening prayers and you can feel the collective surge of community spirit and faith. Many hotels and cafes erect colourful tents for the whole month, and Bahrainis and expatriates alike gather to socialise, eat and play a range of traditional games like backgammon. Ramadan ends with a three-day holiday and celebration, Eid Al Fitr, the Feast of the Breaking of the Fast. The other main celebration is Eid Al Adha, the Feast of the Sacrifice, which marks the end of the annual Hajj pilgrimage to Mecca.

National Dress

Most Bahrainis wear traditional dress, which consists of a long sleeved, floor length thobe or dishdasha for men. This is almost always white, although in winter months, navy blue and brown are common. On their heads they wear a white crocheted skull cap covered by a white cloth, called a gutra, folded into a triangle and topped by a black double-ringed agal, which was originally the rope with which camels were hobbled. The agal holds the gutra in place. Sometimes, particularly in winter, a red and white checked gutra is worn, but the white one is more common in Bahrain. For special occasions, sheikhs or important businessmen may also wear a thin black or gold robe, a bisht, over the thobe.

Bahraini women are quite conservative, and while some do not wear the full black abaya, many of them wear the hijaab (head scarf) and clothes that cover their bodies. Some women also wear black stockings and gloves, and thick veils.

Visitors and expatriates are advised to show respect for the local culture when it comes to dress. While sleeveless and tighter-fitting outfits for women are increasingly seen, particularly in clubs and restaurants, it is advisable to dress more modestly in the souks, malls and places where there are a lot of Bahrainis or Asian expatriates, especially if you don't want people staring at you.

Cuisine

As a cosmopolitan country with a large expatriate population, Bahrain offers almost every type of international cuisine. This ranges from the expensive to the very reasonable, so there

really is something to suit every taste and budget. While many restaurants are located in hotels, some of the best restaurants are found in the suburbs. Bahrain's regulations allow restaurants to hold alcohol licences even if they are not part of a hotel, unlike some other places in the Gulf (See Going Out, p.120).

What people refer to as 'local' cuisine in Bahrain is actually a blend of various Middle Eastern cuisines, primarily Lebanese and Iranian, as well as dishes from the Indian subcontinent. The larger hotels serve Arabic food in their main restaurants, including wide-ranging buffets offering all the mezze and salads particular to the region alongside biryanis and machboos (spiced rice dishes cooked with meat or fish).

In addition, you would really miss out if you didn't visit the various stalls selling shawarma (lamb or chicken sliced from a spit and served with tahina sauce and salad in pita bread) and Bahraini

Shisha

Shisha, the water pipe sometimes called a hubbly-bubbly, is smoked throughout the Middle East and Bahrain is no exception. It is a popular pastime, often enjoyed in local cafes while socialising with friends. It's a completely different type of smoking from cigarettes or cigars, as the water smoothes the smoke, for a more soothing effect, and even people who don't smoke should try it at least once. You don't often see Bahraini women smoking in public, but a row of ancient Bahraini grannies sitting on the floor smoking shisha pipes is a common sight at bridal parties. Try Al Berdaouni (p.126) or one of the many cafes in Adliya.

tikka (black-lemon spiced meat served with bread). Food from these stalls is very reasonably priced and represents a large percentage of the 'fastfood' eaten here. There are also numerous juice stalls not be missed. Indulge in a freshly-squeezed juice; cheap, cheerful and refreshing, particularly if you've been traipsing around the souk on a hot day.

Pork is the most stringently taboo food for Muslims, so you don't find it featured widely on menus. That said, it is served in many restaurants catering to westerners, but is clearly marked so that there is no confusion. The taboo extends to the storage, preparation and handling of pork, so restaurants that serve it, or supermarkets that sell it, must have completely separate refrigeration, handling and preparation areas.

The consumption of alcohol is also against Islamic law and forbidden to Muslims to drink or even handle it. However, the attitude to alcohol in Bahrain is far more relaxed than some other parts of the Middle East. Alcohol is served in licensed outlets; these include clubs, restaurants and bars, the latter being required to be associated with a hotel. Alcohol is also sold in licensed booze shops, such as BMMI and Gulf Cellar.

The law states that alcohol may only be sold to non-Muslims, but in practice this is not rigidly enforced and at weekends the car parks outside the alcohol outlets are full of cars with number plates from Bahrain's nearest neighbour. Bahrain is one of the most liberal countries in the GCC, but out of respect for local culture it's advisable not to overly flaunt the consumption of alcohol.

It is also wise to remember that it is illegal to drive after drinking, with a zero tolerance policy process in place.

History

Referred to as the Garden of Eden, with a history as rich as it is old, the story of Bahrain reads like an epic fairytale.

Archaeologists have found that Bahrain has been inhabited for at least the last 7,000 years, with evidence of two distinct civilizations, Dilmun and Tylos, 2,000 years apart.

Dilmun was a Bronze Age trading empire and its strategic position on the Mesopotamia/Indus Valley trade route meant that it became a watering place for ships carrying goods. Soon enough it was considered a strategic trading post with well-developed social systems.

As a spring-watered garden land, Dilmun stood out in contrast to the surrounding deserts. In the Babylonian Epic of Gilgamesh, Dilmun has been described as 'paradise', where there is a constant abundance of sweet water and the brave and the wise enjoy eternal life. Some scholars have suggested that Bahrain may be the site of the biblical Garden of Eden.

Dilmun was absorbed by the Assyrian and Babylonian empires, and in 323BC, the Persian Empire's domination of the region was ended by the arrival of Alexander the Great. Although there is no direct evidence that the Greeks conquered Bahrain specifically, there is definitely strong Greek influence starting with its new name, Tylos. New trade routes opened and Tylos remained a prosperous trading port within the Greek Empire for the next 600 years.

In the seventh century, Bahrain received a personal invitation from the Prophet Mohammed to convert to Islam, and many of the island's inhabitants did so. In the early 16th century, the Portuguese came through, attracted to the place for its trade relations, pearl exports and boat building industry.

In 1602, an uprising ousted the Portuguese and the islands became part of the Persian Empire. That didn't last too long and by 1783 the Persians were expelled by the Al Khalifa dynasty, Bahrain's current ruling family.

In 1861 Bahrain signed a treaty with Britain, who offered protection from the Ottomans in exchange for unlimited access to the Gulf. Oil was discovered in the 1930s and just in time, with the development of the Japanese cultured pearl industry - the world's natural pearl market was collapsing, so the oil money was a very welcome source of income. The British Empire took note, and the main British naval base in the region was moved to Bahrain in 1935, with the senior British official in the Middle East following in 1946. The 1950s saw an increase

The Development Of Islam

The religion developed in modern-day Saudi Arabia at the beginning of the seventh century AD with the revelations of the Quran being received by the Prophet Mohammed. Military conquests of the Middle East and North Africa enabled the Arab empire to spread the teachings of Islam from Mecca and Medina to the local Bedouin tribes.

in anti-British sentiment and the rise of Arab nationalism led to the announcement by Britain of its intention to leave the Gulf. Bahrain finally proclaimed its independence on August 14, 1971.

As the price of oil rocketed during the 1970s and 1980s, Bahrain developed in great strides. It also capitalised on its superior level of development and education to make it the region's centre for banking. Despite the Gulf-wide economic downturn of the late '80s, Bahrain remained relatively prosperous.

In 2001, reforms intended to transform the country into a constitutional monarchy were proposed and supported overwhelmingly by Bahrainis. The following year, elections were held for a 40 member parliament, the Council of Deputies, a dozen of whom are Shia. This was the first poll in nearly 30 years, since the National Assembly was dissolved in 1975. Since then, the country has enjoyed increasing freedom of expression and an improvement in human rights.

As part of the reform process, the 12 administrative areas, which had little autonomy, have been consolidated into five autonomous municipal areas. The new law has given the municipalities administrative and financial autonomy and clearly demarcated their responsibilities over public spaces, roads, beaches and the environment.

Bahrain has excellent relations with its neighbours and the rest of the world. Since the long-running battle with Qatar over the Hawar islands, it has not been involved in any international disputes and generally takes a neutral stance on global affairs.

Bahrain Timeline

500BC	Evidence of Bahrain's earliest civilisation; the empire of Dilmun (Bronze Age)
323BC	Absorbed by the Assyrian and Babylonian empires
7AD	Bahrain converts to Islam
1500s	Invaded and colonised by the Portuguese
1602	Portuguese are ousted by the Persians who regain control again
1783	Persians expelled by the Al Khalifa family, current ruling family
1861	Treaty of perpetual peace and friendship with Britain
1971	Declaration of Independence and new treaty of friendship with Britain
1986	King Fahd Causeway opened between Bahrain and Saudi Arabia
1992	Establishment of the Shura (Consultative) Council
1999	Sheikh Hamad bin Isa Al Khalifa's accession
2001	National Action Charter: Bahrainis vote for constitutional monarchy (the emir became king)
2002	First municipal elections held

Bahrain Today

With its neighbours moving onwards and upwards, Bahrain has never been one to lag behind. Hold on to your hats, this is going to get big!

Bahrain is currently undergoing rapid expansion and there are a number of exciting retail, business, and commercial and property developments on the horizon. There are islands, residential complexes and financial developments all currently under construction or in the planning stage so if you're planning to see yesterday's Bahrain you better catch it today.

As the capital city, Manama stands as the centre for government, the diplomatic community, business, entertainment and shopping. It doubles up as an incredible area, rich in history, but its development over the past 20 years has resulted in an ultra-modern metropolis with continuous construction changing its skyline. New developments, which seem to spring up overnight, are an omnipresent feature of the city. Projects to look out for include Durrat Al Bahrain in the south of the island; a residential and leisure complex and the Financial Harbour in Manama which will attract even more business into the area.

Tourism received a major boost with the opening of the Bahrain International Circuit in 2004, the first ever in the region. Approximately 30,000 people attended the first Grand Prix with most of the foreign visitors coming from Europe, all vying for the best hotel rooms in Manama. Further information on tourism in Bahrain can be found at www.bahrain.com.

Index

Index

Explorer Products

Residents' Guides

All you need to know about living, working and enjoying life in these exciting destinations

Mini Guides

Perfect pocket-sized
visitors' guides

Activity Guides

Drive, trek, dive and swim... life will never be boring again

Mini Maps

Fit the city in your pocket

Maps

Wherever you are, never get lost again

* Covers not final; titles released second quarter 2008

Photography Books

Beautiful cities caught through the lens.

Lifestyle Products & Calendars

The perfect accessories for a buzzing lifestyle

Explorer Team

Publisher
Alistair MacKenzie
Associate Publisher Claire England

Editorial
Group Editor Jane Roberts
Lead Editors David Quinn,
Matt Farquharson, Sean Kearns, Tim
Binks, Tom Jordan
Deputy Editors Helen Spearman, Jakob
Marsico, Katie Drynan, Pamela Afram,
Richard Greig, Tracy Fitzgerald
Senior Editorial Assistant
Mimi Stankova
Editorial Assistants Grace Carnay,
Ingrid Cupido, Kathryn Calderon

Design
Creative Director Pete Maloney
Art Director Ieyad Charaf
Design Manager Alex Jeffries
Senior Designer Iain Young
Layout Manager Jayde Fernandes
Designers Hashim Moideen, Rafi Pullat,
Shawn Jackson Zuzarte
Cartography Manager Zainudheen
Madathil
Cartographers Noushad Madathil,
Sunita Lakhiani
Design Admin Manager
Shyrell Tamayo
Production Coordinator Maricar Ong

Photography
Photography Manager Pamela Grist
Photographer Victor Romero
Image Editor Henry Hilos

Sales & Marketing
Media Sales Area Managers
Laura Zuffa, Stephen Jones
GCC Retail Sales Manager
Michael Dominic
Global Partners Sales Manager
Andrew Burgess
Corporate Sales Executive Ben Merrett
Marketing Manager Kate Fox
Marketing Executive Annabel Clough
Digital Content Manager
Derrick Pereira
International Retail Sales Manager
Ivan Rodrigues
Retail Sales Coordinator Kiran Melwani
Retail Sales Supervisor Mathew Samuel
Retail Sales Merchandisers
Johny Mathew, Shan Kumar
Sales & Marketing Coordinator
Lennie Mangalino
Distribution Executives Ahmed
Mainodin, Firos Khan, Mannie Lugtu
Warehouse Assistants Mohammed
Kunjaymo, Najumudeen K.I.
Drivers Mohammed Sameer,
Shabsir Madathil

Finance & Administration
Finance Manager Michael Samuel
HR & Administration Manager
Andrea Fust
Junior Accountant Cherry Enriquez
Accounts Assistant Darwin Lovitos
Administrators Enrico Maullon, Joy
Tuborg, Kelly Tesoro
Driver Rafi Jamal

IT
IT Administrator Ajay Krishnan
Senior Software Engineer
Bahrudeen Abdul
Software Engineer Roshni Ahuja

Contact Us

▶ **Reader Response**
If you have any comments and suggestions, fill out
our online reader response form and you could win prizes.
Log on to **www.explorerpublishing.com**

▶ **General Enquiries**
We'd love to hear your thoughts and answer any questions
you have about this book or any other Explorer product.
Contact us at **Info@explorerpublishing.com**

▶ **Careers**
If you fancy yourself as an Explorer, send your CV (stating the
position you're interested in) to **Jobs@explorerpublishing.com**

▶ **Designlab and Contract Publishing**
For enquiries about Explorer's Contract Publishing arm and
design services contact **Designlab@explorerpublishing.com**

▶ **Maps**
For cartography enquries, including orders and comments,
contact **Maps@explorerpublishing.com**

▶ **Corporate Sales**
For bulk sales and customisation options, for this book or any
Explorer product, contact **Sales@explorerpublishing.com**

Explorer Publishing & Distribution
www.explorerpublishing.com

Contributing Authors
Brig Rooke, Edel Moroney, Maureen Spencer,
Rory Adamson & Susie Spratt

EXPLORER